C0-DKN-731

Library of
Davidson College

New England
Off the Beaten Path

Corinne Madden Ross
and Ralph Woodward

917.4
R823w

Copyright 1981 by Fast & McMillan Publishers, Inc.

First printing.

All rights reserved. No part of this book may be reproduced without permission from the publisher, except by a reviewer who may quote brief passages in a review; nor may any part of this book be reproduced, stored in a retrieval system or transmitted in any form or by any means, electronic, mechanical, photocopying, recording or other, without permission from the publisher.

Library of Congress Cataloging in Publication Data

Ross, Corinne Madden.
    New England, off the beaten path.

    Includes index.
    1. New England—Description and travel—1951—Guide-books. I. Woodward, Ralph, 1930-   joint author. II. Title.
F2.3.R67   917.4'0443   80-27933
ISBN 0-914788-40-X (pbk.)

Cover design by Bill Bradford
Map by Joel Tevebaugh
Type by Raven Type
Printed in the United States of America

The East Woods Press
Fast & McMillan Publishers, Inc.
820 East Boulevard
Charlotte, NC 28203

81-8598

Table of Contents

Off the Beaten Path in New England

Massachusetts
1. Beverly
2. Rockport
3. Boston
4. Cambridge
5. Waban
6. Framingham

Rhode Island
7. Newport
8. Westerly
9. Arcadia
10. Providence

Vermont
11. St. Johnsbury
12. Montpelier
13. Burlington
14. Cuttingsville
15. Norwich

New Hampshire
16. Lake Winnepesaukee
17. Melvin Village
18. Laconia
19. Ashland
20. Harrisville

Connecticut
21. Greenwich
22. Stamford
23. Norwalk—South Norwalk
24. Willimantic

Maine
25. Cape Neddick
26. Portland
27. South Paris
28. Camden
29. Rockland
30. Damariscotta
? Milfred

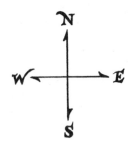

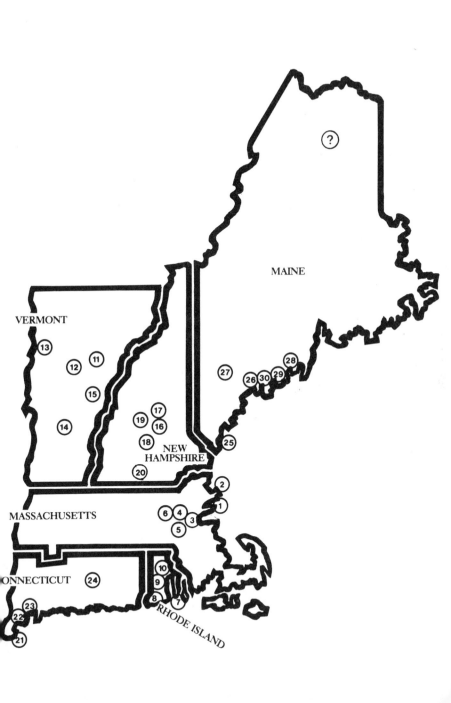

Introduction

New England: Off the Beaten Path is not meant to be a guidebook in the conventional sense. It is intended for the adventuresome traveler who enjoys seeking out back roads, hidden corners, the eccentric and unusual, and excellence in unpromising or unexpected surroundings. Most of the restaurants, museums, shops, scenic drives, parks, historic houses, inns and the like described in the book are not generally listed elsewhere. To some residents of a given area, of course, many of the listings will be familiar. But for anyone else they will come, we hope, as pleasant surprises.

This book reflects our own tastes and partialities; it is a very personal collection of places to go and things to see or do. If any reader finds fault with our descriptions (or choices) we wish to state here and now that we take no responsibility for any of them! We have tried to be as accurate as possible in providing directions, hours and days open, prices, etc. Occasionally, however, situations or ownerships change; rates or prices may increase; restaurants, inns and shops may change hands or even go out of business; a scenic drive may disappear under a new superhighway. If any of these calamities should occur, we apologize in advance.

In researching the book we explored countless byways throughout the six-state New England region. Sometimes we tracked down leads provided by friends or local inhabitants, and we would like to take this opportunity to thank all of those helpful people who contributed ideas or recommendations. But the majority of the places described we found on our own, and that is what the book is really all about—the pleasure of unexpected discoveries. In *New England: Off the Beaten Path*, we have included a broad sampling of our favorite finds, and we hope that you will be challenged to search out even more.

A good way to begin searching on your own is to acquire a detailed map of an area and follow any of the multitudes of back roads shown. Another, and often the best method, is to ignore maps entirely and just wander. Although it takes a dash of pioneer spirit to leave the security of the highways, the venture is well worth the risk. You may get lost, but usually the road will eventually lead you to a town or marked crossroad. If not, you can always retrace your steps and start over. And whenever you are in a town or city, by all means ask the residents for suggestions. New Englanders are friendly folk; their cool reputation is undeserved and, if given a chance, they will be delighted to share their knowledge of an area with you.

Someone once commented that *all* of New England is off the beaten path, and in some ways it is. The six states (Connecticut, Rhode Island, Massachusetts, New Hampshire, Vermont and Maine) offer seemingly endless sources of surprise, and it would take several lifetimes to ferret them all out. *New England: Off the Beaten Path* is designed to get you started. We think you'll find the quest rewarding, and a great deal of fun. As one newfound friend mused when replying to our questions about her town: "Off the beaten path sounds like a fine place to live!"

Off the Beaten Path in Connecticut

The Greenwich Area

Traveling engenders healthy appetites, and your authors may as well admit right at the start that they enjoy good food. They also confess to a fondness for bake shops.

In Greenwich, down in Connecticut's southeastern corner, the main street offers not one but two excellent bakeries—located only a block apart. The **Versailles**, at 315 Greenwich Avenue, and the **St. Moritz Patisserie** at No. 383, are both superb. The Versailles is the newer of the two, and includes a small dining area where you may order coffee or tea to go along with your choice of pastry. The attractive china menu also offers pates, quiche, escargots and other light selections. Glass display cases show off a host of culinary marvels; one fanciful item that caught our eye was a cake resembling a giant, dusky chocolate rose. We opted for tarts, however—one apricot and one creamy lemon creation. The verdict: delicious, especially the latter.

The St. Moritz, a bakery only, has an even larger assortment of wares. Handsomely decorated cakes, tarts, and cookies of all kinds including chocolate leaves and Florentines, are for sale. Here we carefully selected an eclair and a deliciously drippy rum baba. As we were leaving, another customer smiled at us and commented, "Isn't this a wonderful place? I come here all the way from Long Island!"

If you are feeling exceptionally self-indulgent, wander across the street to an establishment called **Pinguino, Inc.** Pinguino, a *gelateria* (*gelato* is Italian for ice cream), is connected with the famed shop of the same name in Florence, Italy. That award-winning gelateria has been in business for more than 80 years and is owned and operated by the president of the Italian Ice Cream Makers' Society. The Greenwich shop belongs to Lynn C. Winther, M.D., who is related to the Italian Pinguinos. The products are all made on the premises using recipes and equipment identical to those in Florence.

Pinguino claims to be the only place in the United States where one can find genuine, all-natural Italian gelato and *semifreddo* (a rich dessert made with heavy cream similar to a frozen mousse). The bright, airy ice cream parlor, decorated with fresh flowers and plants, also offers *cappucino, espresso, chocolatino,* pastries, herbal teas, sodas, shakes and sundaes—all made with natural ingredients of the highest quality. Even the fruit flavors come from freshly squeezed fruit juices, not from concentrates or extracts.

Pinguino, Inc. is located at 368 Greenwich Avenue, Greenwich, CT (203)661-6347. Hours are: Tuesday through Thursday from 12 noon-10 p.m., Friday and Saturday from 12 noon-11 p.m.; closed on Sunday.

Getting away from the interesting topic of food for a moment, there is an unusually appealing stationery shop in Greenwich called **Therese Saint Clair,** named for its owner. On one side of the shop is a large selection of personalized and packaged stationery plus an international selection of note cards and related paper items. On the other side you'll find a collection of handsome leather items, gifts, prints, and English antique collectibles. The tall cabinets, 100-year-old decorative tin ceiling, stained glass windows and colorful displays create an inviting atmosphere for browsing.

Therese Saint Clair, 23 Lewis Street (off upper Greenwich Avenue), Greenwich, CT (203)661-2927, is open Monday through Saturday, 9:30 a.m.-5:30 p.m. Visa and MasterCard are accepted.

Greenwich also offers a really nice small bookshop—**Just Books, Inc.** Warren Cassell's shop is a low-keyed, old-fashioned establishment where the customer is treated with care and affection, and by name, if possible. Mr. Cassell says that Just Books does *not* have "piped-in music, computerized billing, illiterate clerks or junk mass market paperbacks." He adds: "We *do* have an exceptionally fine line of books. They, plus our other qualities, attract those seeking elegance, personal service, and a complete absence of vulgarity . . . a felicitous group including artists, authors, statesmen and others possessing a quiet celebrity."

Just Books is situated at 19 East Putnam Avenue (Rte. 1), Greenwich, CT 06830 (203)869-5023. (On the Post Road between Greenwich Avenue and Mason Street.) Open weekdays from 9 a.m.-5:30 p.m.; Saturdays from 9 a.m.-5 p.m.; closed Sundays. No credit cards; personal checks or charges are just fine.

If you have followed our lead and sampled some of Greenwich's pastries and/or ice cream, you may feel the need for more exercise than exploring the town's many shops will provide. In that case, nearby Cos Cob (part of Greenwich) has the perfect spot for walking off calories. **The Montgomery Pinetum** is a really beautiful woodland park with rare conifers, nature trails, wild flowers, and exceptional plantings of azaleas, bulbs and primroses.

A "pinetum," by the way, is exactly what it sounds like: "a planting of pine trees, especially for botanical studies." The late Colonel Robert H. Montgomery bequeathed the 61-acre property to the community of Greenwich "as a public park or garden for the pleasure and education of the public at large." There are picnic tables and restrooms not far from the parking area.

Also on the grounds is the **Greenwich Garden Center,** with a gardening and horticulture information service and a lending library of horticultural and flower arranging books. The gift shop offers flower arranging equipment, hard-to-find containers, a variety of unusual note paper, pot holders, cache pots, and much more. There is also a greenhouse, and in May the Center sponsors a market offering choice wild flowers, vegetables, herbs, hanging baskets and pottery for sale. Lunch is served on the terrace during the May Market and there are art exhibits and flower shows, too.

The Montgomery Pinetum (with ponds, brooks, gardens and hemlock groves) and the Greenwich Garden Center are on Bible Street, Cos Cob, CT (203)869-9242. Directions: From Rte. 1 (E. Putnam Avenue) take a left onto Orchard Street (see the sign for the Greenwich Garden Center) and bear right on Bible Street (about three-quarters of a mile). The Pinetum is open daily during daylight hours, and a map of the grounds is available at the Garden Center. The Garden Center is open 9 a.m.-4 p.m. Monday through Friday from September through June, in July from 9 a.m.-12 noon; closed during August.

Greenwich Point, once a pair of islands, is another magnificent park in the Greenwich area. Unfortunately, it is open to the general public only from December through March; the rest of the year admission is limited to local residents. But if you're in Old Greenwich during the winter months, try not to miss it. Drive along the winding road or hike over some of the trails; you'll find everything from sweeping ocean vistas to a holly grove with twenty-one varieties of the red-berried bush.

J. Kennedy Tod, a wealthy banker, purchased the Point in

11

1889 and named it "Innis Arden." The foundation of his mansion still remains, on the opposite side of the big lagoon. Greenwich has owned the property since 1944. The 147 acres include coastal marsh, a half-mile-long sandy beach, rocky strands, salt ponds, a brackish lake, fields and woods. The park also offers picnicking and boating facilities. Small animals live on the Point in large numbers, and the visitor may see a great many species of birds including egrets, herons, Canada geese, ducks and gulls.

To reach the Point from Old Greenwich, follow the main street (Sound Beach Avenue) south to Shore Road and turn right, a total distance of about two miles.

The **Cafe du Bec Fin** in Old Greenwich is, happily, open year-round. Located right on the main street, it is an elegant little bistro specializing in nouvelle cuisine. Owned by French-trained chef Harvey Edwards, Cafe du Bec Fin is expensive, especially if you order one of the choice wines that are available. But the food is superb—each dish individually prepared and deftly served. As the menu is changed every two weeks, we won't recommend any particular item. Suffice it to say that anything you choose, from soup or appetizer through irresistible dessert accompanied by excellent coffee, will be well worth the price.

Cafe du Bec Fin is at 199 Sound Beach Avenue, Old Greenwich, CT (203)637-4447. Lunch is served from 12 noon-2 p.m. Tuesday through Friday; dinner is served from 6-10 p.m. Monday through Friday and to 11 p.m. on Saturday. Closed Sunday. Reservations are advisable for lunch and required for dinner. Visa, MasterCard and American Express are accepted.

For travelers who enjoy staying in an historic old house instead of a hotel or motel, we recommend **The Homestead Inn** in Greenwich. The building, which dates from 1799, was originally a New England farmhouse. It was the homestead of Augustus I. Mead, a judge and gentleman farmer. Mead's ancestors were among the 28 early settlers who, in 1672, purchased what is now the town of Greenwich from the Indians of the Misehassky tribe. In 1859, the house was sold to innkeepers who remodeled it in the distinctive "Carpenter Gothic" style of the Victorian era. Back around the turn of the century, Greenwich boasted eleven inns; the Homestead is the only one remaining today.

Lessie Davison and Nancy K. Smith purchased the inn in

1978; after carefully restoring and renovating the building, they reopened it the following year. Be sure to ask your hostesses to tell you about the renovation project—it's a fascinating story. Always a quiet, peaceful haven, the inn once again offers an unpretentious, relaxed ambiance, with a great deal of charm.

There are 13 rooms for guests, each one different. All are corner rooms with private baths, electric blankets, hemstitched sheets, clock-radios, phones, color TVs and many antiques. Each room has its own name, too: "The Bride's Room," "The Sleigh-Bed Room," and the like. Guests are invited to make use of the pleasant lounge with fireplace, a backgammon room with green felt walls and another fireplace, and—in warm weather—the old-fashioned porch with comfortable wicker chairs.

The cozy Chocolate Bar serves generous drinks, and fine French cuisine is offered in **La Grange**, a handsome dining room with rugged barn siding, massive ancient chestnut beams, a skylight and a fireplace. House specialties (prepared by the French chef) include Pate de Saumon, Gratin de Fruits de Mer, Poularde aux Morilles, Tournedo Beauvillon and Rognon de Veau Beauge, flavored with herbs from the inn's own kitchen garden.

Set among old trees and broad lawns in a gracious residential area to the west of Greenwich Harbor, the Homestead Inn is a short drive from Greenwich's main street with its many interesting shops. The ocean (Long Island Sound) is nearby, too, and in summers a town-operated ferry will take you over to Island Beach.

The Homestead Inn is located at 420 Field Point Road, Greenwich, CT 06830 (203)869-7500. It is a little tricky to find, so we suggest you ask in town or telephone the inn for directions. The Homestead Inn is open year-round. La Grange restaurant is open for luncheon and dinner, and a Continental breakfast is available for guests staying at the inn. Prices for both inn and restaurant are fairly high.

Stamford

Most people enjoy scavenging through flea markets, yard or rummage sales, even town dumps, searching for the odd, the unusual or the useful. In Stamford, Connecticut, **The United House Wrecking Company** offers an assortment of objects so vast as to be virtually indescribable. But we'll try.

Off The Beaten Path in . . .

The place has been called "a junkyard with a personality," which may give you an inkling of what to expect.

A fish weathervane; a 1920s vintage raccoon coat, not too scruffy, for $200; a brass spittoon; an enormous crystal chandelier for $1500.

In 1954, three brothers (Philip, Ron and John Lodato) and Ray Bowling, their brother-in-law, formed the company. They began by demolishing houses, but eventually gave up that aspect of the business to concentrate on selling items acquired from a broad network of sources: other wreckers, houses undergoing renovation, marine salvage, etc. Their establishment is a decorator's dream come true, a farrago of architectural fragments such as cornices, moldings, mantels and doors—all crafted in a bygone era when fine workmanship (and materials) were affordable. But these classic offerings are only the beginning.

The Homestead Inn. Greenwich, CT.

An aquarium coffee table complete with live goldfish swimming about, old farm tools and wagons, a working traffic light for your very own.

Imagine, if you can, six acres of THINGS. Any acquisitive instinct lurking within your soul will be aroused to fever pitch by the sight of this sprawling collection of antiques, relics, memorabilia of the past, odds and ends, and just plain junk.

Statuary and cast-iron garden benches, seemingly endless rows of brass and glassware, a venerable milk wagon, a church steeple topped by an eagle weathervane.

Phil Lodato, an affable, enthusiastic gentlemen, told us that the range of prices for items on the grounds runs from 10¢ to around $20,000 (the latter for an exceptionally fine stained glass window). Lodato and his partners don't, as one might assume, collect pieces to hold onto for their increasing value. On the contrary, they believe in a fast turnover—United House Wrecking simply buys and sells. And on any given day there is no telling what you might find.

A small stuffed animal (species unknown) perched on a step-ladder; a handsome church confessional, all yours for $1200; a life-sized mastiff sculpture at $250; a pinball machine; an oak dining table.

It's all great fun to see, and examining even a portion of it takes time. The wares, tasteful to tacky, are displayed both indoors and out. There are several rambling buildings stuffed to the rafters; outside, visitors wander past stacks of doors, piles of architectural what's-its, a rocky hillside "garden" of statuary, and innumerable large objects of all kinds. The sheer number of things is bewildering, but if you are looking for a particular item, just ask any of the cashiers—or one of the owners. They know, somehow, where everything is.

A ship's wheel or brass rail, a Tiffany-style lamp, a magnificent ship's figurehead, an authentic New York City subway car (The 8th Ave. Local).

Some 300,000 people find their way to the United House Wrecking Company each year, some bent on serious buying, others just to look. We confidently predict that you'll find the place memorable. One word of caution: there is the sad possibility of the company having to give up its present (and very valuable) location. The owners have not yet decided whether or not to try to move—an enormously difficult project. As we go to press all is well, but we advise that you

15

telephone ahead of time, just to make sure they are still there.

The United House Wrecking Company is located at 328 Selleck Street, Stamford, CT (203)348-5371. From I-95, take Exit 6; turn right on West Avenue to the rotary, then right on Belleck Street—you can't miss it. Open from 9 a.m.-5 p.m. Tuesday through Saturday; closed Sunday and Monday. Visa, MasterCard and American Express cards are accepted.

While you're in Stamford, perhaps you would like to meet an otter. There are two of the winsome creatures at the **Stamford Museum and Nature Center.** The male, in particular, is fond of visitors. The otters may be found in their own outdoor enclosure adjacent to a large pond abounding with ducks, geese and swans, and a farm with animals to pet and feed.

The Museum is a unique combination of farm, wildlife zoo, art gallery, natural history museum, nature trails, observatory and planetarium—all on 118 acres of New England woods and fields. Nature and art classes are offered regularly, as well as folk music concerts. One of the nature programs offered recently was called "Owl Prowl." A slide show about owls was followed by a tour of nesting areas during which the museum lecturer attempted to entice the birds from their hiding places with his owl calls.

The Stamford Museum and Nature Center is at 39 Scofieldtown Road, Stamford, CT (203)322-1646. Take Exit 35 from Rte. 15 (Merritt Parkway) and travel north about one mile on High Ridge Road to Scofieldtown Road. Open Monday through Saturday 9 a.m.-5 p.m., Sunday 1 p.m.-5 p.m. (From November to March, Monday hours are also from 1 p.m.-5 p.m.)

Norwalk/South Norwalk

Have you ever considered the effect that background music has on your enjoyment of (or disenchantment with) a restaurant meal? John Grasso has.

Grasso, a sometime musician, is the manager of **Loaves & Fishes,** an excellent small seafood restaurant in Norwalk, Connecticut. Not long after he began working there, he noticed an air of boredom about the place and came to the conclusion that the music was to blame. It certainly wasn't the food! So he put together a series of tapes—an eclectic blend of sea chanteys, folk, classical and contemporary sounds. And it worked. Don't get the wrong idea, though; the music is never obtrusive. It is there, you hear it, but the impact is subliminal. As a diner you simply feel relaxed and very pleased with your surroundings.

Loaves & Fishes was opened in 1979 by Frank Laurino and his wife Jo-Anne. Laurino, who had been in marketing, loved to cook and wanted an opportunity to express his talents. The restaurant's slogan is: "Delightful Atmosphere ... Delicious Fishes." It is, and they are. So is everything else, including a marvelous cheddar cheese soup, the pepperoni and spinach bread and the thinnest of French fried onion rings. In addition to the regular menu, a blackboard lists daily specials. Bay Scallops Oriental is a favorite of manager Grasso's. Even if it's not on when you are there, ask him to describe it—his enthusiastic recital of the ingredients is irresistible.

Desserts, except for the cheesecake, are homemade and incorporate unique touches like using Kahlua instead of vanilla in the pecan pie. Even the coffees and drinks (including Fish House Punch) have personality. The "Whitecap," an after-dinner concoction of hazelnut liqueur topped with cream sprinkled with nutmeg, is particularly delectable. The selection of beers is outstanding, too, and the restaurant promotes a different wine each week with a printed description of its history and qualities.

Loaves & Fishes is a friendly, informal restaurant. Bread wreaths decorated with plaid ribbons adorn the walls, along with color photos of undersea scenes. There are fresh flowers, in Pernod bottles, on each table. It is the kind of place that people adopt—a "participatory" restaurant to which patrons return time and time again to check out the latest menu innovations and, often, to suggest new recipes for chef-owner Laurino to try.

Loaves & Fishes is located at 456 Main Avenue (Rte. 7), Norwalk, CT (203)846-0022. From the Merritt Parkway take Exit 40 and follow Rte. 7 for half a mile; the restaurant is in a small shopping mall opposite Merritt 7, a large office complex. Lunch is served daily from 11:30 a.m.-2:30 p.m.; dinner is served from 5:30 p.m.-9:30 p.m. weekdays, to 10 or 10:30 p.m. weekends. Reservations are advisable unless you don't mind waiting in line. Prices are moderate. Visa, MasterCard and American Express are accepted.

Still on the pleasant subjects of food and drink, let us tell you about **Jeremiah Donovan's,** a classic old-time saloon down on South Norwalk's historic waterfront. Donovan, a former mayor of Norwalk, established the place in 1889 and it has been operating ever since. According to hosts Richard Ball and Tom Kibbe, Presidential candidates all the way back to Theodore Roosevelt have stopped in for a drink or a meal at Donovan's while campaigning in the area.

The South Norwalk waterfront, with its fine collection of structures dating back to the mid-1800s and early 1900s, is in the initial stages of an ambitious restoration program. Plans are in the works to refurbish the buildings and install brick paving, period street lights, trees and pedestrian walkways. Donovan's, a vital part of the restoration, is located on the first floor of a handsome three-story building. The high-ceilinged saloon boasts an antique mahogany bar and authentic brass rail; the walls are covered with old photographs of prizefighters and other boxing memorabilia. The drinks are generous and the fare is plain and hearty: beef stew, chowder and chili, sandwiches, seafood and roast beef. Homemade desserts may include French chocolate mocha cake and apple walnut pie. Families are most welcome, and prices are moderate.

Jeremiah Donovan's is at 138 Washington Street, South Norwalk, (203)838-3430. From I-95 take Exit 15 south to North Main Street, then left on Washington; Donovan's is at the end of the block at the corner of Water Street, adjacent to the waterfront. The restaurant is open Monday through Saturday for lunch and dinner from 12 noon-3 p.m. and 6 p.m.-10 p.m. The bar is open daily from 11:30 a.m.-1 a.m., Friday and Saturday nights to 2 a.m. Visa and MasterCard are accepted.

On the edge of South Norwalk's revitalization project, there is another good place to eat called **Hugo's Again.** Hugo Vogt began a family tradition of restaurants in 1919 in his native Germany. Following World War I he came to the United States and operated several restaurants over the years in Connecticut's Stamford area. Then, after Hugo's retirement, his wife Ingeborg formed a partnership with son Raymond and opened a new dining establishment—appropriately named Hugo's Again.

"Gemütlich," German for "cozy and comfortable," is the restaurant's motto. The atmosphere is charmingly old-world with dark wood paneling, exposed beams and brick walls,

Jeremiah Donovan's. South Norwalk, CT.

brightened by plants, mirrors and gleaming touches of brass. In addition to German specialties such as sauerbraten, rinderbrust, schweinerbraten, weiner schnitzel and others, there is also a wide selection of American offerings. Several evenings each week diners are entertained by Rozsika and Laszlo, a talented Hungarian couple who play the violin and piano. On other nights, musical performances are given by small local groups or soloists.

Hugo's Again is located at 70 North Main Street, South Norwalk, (203)838-1776. There is a municipal parking lot adjacent. The restaurant is open for lunch Monday through Saturday from 12 noon-3 p.m.; dinner is served Monday through Thursday from 5 p.m.-10 p.m., Friday and Saturday from 5 p.m.-11 p.m. On Sunday, brunch is offered from 12 noon-3 p.m., and dinner from 4 p.m.-9 p.m. A family buffet is also offered on Sunday from 4:30 p.m.-8 p.m. Prices are moderate. MasterCard, Visa and American Express are accepted.

Travelers who wish to take home an unusual souvenir of their journey might consider choosing a bottle of wine at **Elmer's**. This admirable establishment not only offers an exceptional list of fine wines but has a small vineyard out back as well!

Owner Don Singewald, a delightful gentleman, will take anyone who is interested on a tour of the place. He calls it "giving visitors the old razzle dazzle" and it's not only fun, it is educational. He will show you his hybrid French and American vines, plus a few vines brought directly from Burgundy. The latter bore fruit for the first time in the summer of 1980, an impressive feat for a French grape in Connecticut Yankee soil.

Singewald is a mine of information about wine and winemaking and he's the first to admit that he will carry on unchecked for hours if given an audience. Feel free to interrupt, however, and ask him to recommend a bottle or two from the vast assortment available. You might choose a 1976 Moulin des Graves for about $7, a 1977 Chambolle-Musigny for under $20, or—if you really want to impress your friends—a 1966 Mouton Rothschild for $98.75. Currently, Elmer's exclusive Bouchet Blanc and Rouge table wine is the best value around at only $2.99 a bottle.

Customers are offered a 10% discount on mixed purchases over $60 and on mixed or full cases. Should you be interested, that Mouton Rothschild sells for $1,066.50 a case. Elmer's also offers an enormous selection of California wines, and a full range of liquors.

If all of this oenological chitchat has made you hungry as well as thirsty, **"A Little Something"** next door is a pleasant spot to have a bite of food and a glass of wine. The entrance is under a tree at the back of the building, and the restaurant looks out over the vineyard.

Elmer's and "A Little Something" are located on Rte. 7 at the Norwalk/Wilton line.

Georgetown/West Redding

Also on Rte. 7, about six miles beyond Elmer's, there is a super sandwich shop called **Connies' Lunchbox.** It's so small you might easily miss it, and believe us, you don't want to! Watch for the sign and a tiny, rather shabby building painted white with red trim. If you are traveling north towards Danbury, Connies' is on the lefthand side of the road, right at the Wilton/Georgetown line. If you pass the Old Stone Mill hot dog stand, you've gone too far.

Connies' spotless interior, with blue and white checked curtains, a shelf of old-fashioned kitchen implements, and a pot of African violets in the window, has no seats or tables. The shop is purely a take-out establishment, operated by Constance Hubbell and Constance Blain. The two Connies, who once catered for church suppers, joined forces in January, 1978. Connies' Lunchbox, they say, came about when they realized that "there were hungry souls out there who needed a good, substantial lunch and/or breakfast to go—and we filled the need." Their food is so good that lines often form at lunchtime.

Everything is freshly made: large, liberally-filled sandwiches (the Reubens and Rachels are renowned); great salads; homemade soups, different each day, and marvelous desserts including big homemade cookies, cheesecake and daily specials such as apple crisp with whipped cream. Be sure to try the Connies' clam chowder—it ranks among the best we've ever tasted.

Connies' Lunchbox is located at 673 Danbury Road (Rte. 7), Georgetown, CT; (203)544-9182. Open Monday through Friday from 6:30 a.m.-4 p.m., Saturday from 7 a.m.-2 p.m.; closed Sunday.

It occurs to us that perhaps readers might be interested in

our method of tracking down some of the off-the-beaten-path places described in this book. Basically, one of us drives while the other jots down notes on directions. In the following example, we are searching for an old-fashioned country store, called **The Country Emporium.** We are on Rte. 7 traveling north and our notes read thusly:

"Exactly 8/10 of a mile north of the Ridgefield town line, bear right at Walpole Woodworkers onto the Simpaug Turnpike. It is a winding country road following along the railroad tracks. Go 1½ miles, then bear right across the railroad bridge and turn sharp left; continue to West Redding Center and bear right on Station Road. Continue half a mile to junction with Unpawaug Road. We are now lost.

"To the left, down the road, there is a sign for the Emporium. It seems to be pointing to the right, so head in that direction. Two miles later, no Emporium. But the scenery is very pretty. Turn around, retrace the way to Station Road, drive back to West Redding Center to ask someone there for directions. Upon arrival, note that The Country Emporium is in plain sight—across the railroad tracks and to the right."

As is now obvious, your authors are not always as alert as they might be. But tooling around on New England country roads is never a waste of time, and often provides interesting and unusual surprises. Getting lost is only one of these. In this case, unless you really want to explore the region, just follow our noted directions as far as West Redding Center—and *stop*.

Connoisseurs of country stores will find this one superior. The Country Emporium, chock-full of marvelous miscellany, is a rambling, rustic old building with a wonderful, old-time flavor. It was originally a cow barn, and many people hereabouts can remember when cows were milked therein. On your way inside look for the battered barrel on the porch with the sign, "Danger—keep away. Baby rattlers!" Fear not; the rattlers are only wooden baby rattles. Another sign requests: "Don't let the cat in."

Few visitors can wander through a country store without finding something they need, or don't need, but want. The Country Emporium offers a lovely clutter of gifts and gadgets for house and kitchen, wheel cheese and gourmet foods, corn dolls and toys of all kinds, lots of wooden items, and a tempting display of penny candy. (Almost penny, that is. Most of the items will run purchasers 3¢ or perhaps a nickel.) The pleasant woman who doles out the sweet stuff told us that children, even in this sophisticated age, suffer real agonies trying to decide how best to spend their allotted quarters.

The **Country Kitchen,** a small restaurant tucked away in an addition to the barn, serves a splendid assortment of good things to eat. Pancakes come plain or you may order buckwheat, bacon chip, blueberry, cheddar cheese, apple chip, banana or corn. There are crepes, too, including chocolate chip with ice cream and sour cream with lingonberries. A favorite with regular customers is the dillyburger, served with sour cream, horseradish and dill sauce on homemade dill-flavored buns. Beverages include old-fashioned Moxie (yes, there really is such a thing!), sarsaparilla (pronounced "sasparilla"), ginger beer and birch beer.

The Country Emporium (Store and Country Kitchen) is located at Station Place, West Redding, CT; (203)938-2484. The Emporium is open year-round Tuesday through Sunday from 10 a.m.-4 p.m.; closed Monday. The Kitchen serves brunch and lunch Saturdays and Sundays from 10 a.m.-3 p.m., weekdays from 11 a.m.-3 p.m.

Willimantic

In Willimantic, east of Hartford on Rte. 6, there is yet another "emporium," of a very different nature. This one is a slightly mad establishment called **Ziesing Brothers' Book Emporium.** An article in the *Hartford Courant* described the place as "a wonderland that looks like something Alice might have stumbled into . . . a cultural phenomenon that is a cross between a literary salon and a Kool-Aid stand."

Michael and Mark Ziesing (who feel a business should be fun as well as, hopefully, profitable) opened their bookstore in 1974 on one floor of a restored Victorian building on Main Street. The shop has since grown into a veritable maze of 17 rooms, on three levels. Rough-hewn wood shelving holds the books, which include a general line of titles with an emphasis on contemporary American and British poetry and small press literature. The science fiction selection is extensive; there's a special section for comics, too, and two rooms of secondhand books. Another room is set aside for Thursday night poetry readings and changing visual art exhibits. The Ziesings also give weekly book reviews on the local radio station and publish (irregularly) a newsletter, plus a "broad-sheet" of photographs and poetry, and poetry postcards and bookmarks.

Ziesing Brothers' is a haven for book lovers, serious buyers and browsers alike. You never know what will turn up and most likely you will get lost in the stacks at least once. It's quite possible that there are customers who have never managed to find their way out and who are happily existing somewhere inside on a diet of glue and old bindings. You might even run into the ghost of a past tenant of the building, looking confused. Ziesing Brothers' Book Emporium is anything but ordinary; Michael and Mark are firm believers in the element of surprise.

Ziesing Brothers' Book Emporium is located at 768 Main Street (Rte. 6), Willimantic, CT 06226; (203)423-5836. MasterCard and Visa are accepted with a $10 minimum purchase. In general, hours are from 10:30 a.m.-7 p.m. in winter and from 9:30 a.m.-5:30 p.m. in summer, open later on Thursday nights; closed on Sunday.

Off the Beaten Path in Rhode Island

Newport/Middletown/Bristol

If you have ever wondered how the state of Rhode Island (which is not an island) got its name, we will now satisfy your curiosity. Aquidneck Island in Narragansett Bay, first discovered in 1524 by the Italian explorer-navigator Giovanni da Verrazano, was renamed Rhode Island (after the Greek isle of Rhodes) a century later. In 1663 King Charles II of England granted a charter to a confederation made up of the region's early settlements. The name given to the colony—and still official today—was Rhode Island and Providence Plantations. Most maps nowadays call Verrazano's original island both Aquidneck *and* Rhode Island. To avoid confusion, we'll call it Aquidneck.

Newport, at the southernmost end of Aquidneck Island, is a charming old Colonial seaport. Its incredible mansions, constructed as "summer cottages" for the unimaginably wealthy in the latter half of the 19th century, are justly renowned. To see them, follow Ocean Drive; you'll pass one after another of these awesome structures, many of which are open to the public. Exposure to so many examples of grandiose architecture may, however, give you a touch of indigestion. Our advice is to head immediately back into Old Newport. There, on the hills above the harbor, you will find a superb collection of chaste early 18th-century houses—some 400 in all. They offer a pleasant contrast to the mansions: a cleansing of the palate, as it were!

In nearby Middletown, the **Norman Bird Sanctuary** is a wonderful place to spend a few hours hiking along wooded trails. From Newport, go east on Memorial Boulevard and bear right on Second Beach Road to Paradise Avenue; then bear right on Hanging Rock Road to Third Beach Road, turn left and watch for the sign.

The sanctuary offers several different wildlife habitats: upland woods, salt marshes and three swamp-ponds, with 15 miles of self-guided nature trails. Many stone walls are still in place on the grounds; some fields are still worked, others are growing back into woods. From Hanging Rock, an immense, 50-foot-high rocky ridge, there is a grand view of Second Beach and the ocean.

The original property was a farm owned by a prominent 19th-century Newport family, the Normans. In 1948, Mabel Norman Cerio set the land aside as a nature preserve, at first under the auspices of the Audubon Society. Today it is operated by a privately-endowed organization, The Friends of the Norman Bird Sanctuary. In recent years more land has been acquired, and the property now extends over 450 acres.

Some 70 species of birds nest here, and 200 species pass through during migration. In addition to bird-watching, visitors may catch a glimpse of a variety of small animals—foxes, raccoons, rabbits and woodchucks. Most of the animals are nocturnal, however, or appear only at dawn or dusk. Usually a few birds and animals will be on view inside or next to the old barn near the sanctuary's entrance. The staff rescues injured or abandoned wildlife and nurses them back to health, freeing them later if possible.

Children, especially, will enjoy the barn. Nearly 200 years old, the building is in the process of being renovated to include a modern office column within but with the original structure still intact and visible. The barn houses a museum with mounted specimens of native birds, an aquarium, a collection of Indian artifacts and another of early American farm tools. There's also a gift shop.

Two friendly and dedicated young people make up the sanctuary staff—Timothy Traver and Delia Clark. They'll answer all your questions and tell you about the place in enthusiastic detail. Environmental education programs are offered regularly, as well as frequent weekend guided tours. There are picnic grounds for summer use, and in winter cross-country ski trails. A Harvest Fair is held at the sanctuary every year on the first weekend in October. The two-day fair includes music, magic, crafts, games and food.

Running the sanctuary is quite an undertaking for two people, but Traver and Clark are aided by volunteers who help with clearing the trails and general maintenance. Volunteers also assist with the educational programs and other events. More willing workers are always needed, though, so the services of any interested readers will be more than welcome.

The Norman Bird Sanctuary is on Third Beach Road, Middletown, RI 02840 (401)846-2577. It is open year-round Wednesday through Sunday, 9 a.m.-5 p.m. Admission: adults (18 and over) $1, children accompanied by an adult free.

If you would like to explore even more nature trails, the **Sachuest Point National Wildlife Sanctuary** borders the Norman Bird Sanctuary. Another local site of interest is **Purgatory Chasm,** on Purgatory Road. An impressive sight, the chasm is a 160-foot-long cleft in the rock ledges, formed by the eroding action of the sea. And not far away, on Indian Avenue, is **Boothden.** A large, rambling house, Boothden was built in 1883 by the famed Shakespearean actor Edwin Booth, whose brother John Wilkes assassinated President Abraham Lincoln in 1865. The house is privately owned, not open to the public.

Bristol, another picturesque Colonial town, is about 10 miles north of Middletown. To reach it, follow Rte. 114 over the Mt. Hope Bridge. The village was established in 1680 by four Massachusetts investors who saw the potential for a thriving seaport in the deep, sheltered harbor. Bristol's merchants prospered from the first, amassing large fortunes chiefly from the lucrative slave trade—transporting slaves from Africa to the Southern colonies and to West Indian plantations. By the early 1800s, Bristol had become the fourth busiest port in America. But its days of maritime glory were numbered: the slave trade was abolished, and the merchant fleet of tall-masted brigs and schooners was made obsolete by the invention of the steamboat.

In later years Bristol won a new measure of fame as the site of the Herreshoff Boatyard. Here the famed Herreshoff brothers designed and built sleek racing yachts, including every defender of the America's Cup from 1893 to 1934. Yacht engines, fittings, photographs and memorabilia of "The Golden Age of Yachting" are on display at the **Herreshoff Marine Museum,** 18 Burnside Street. The museum is open May to October on Wednesdays and Sundays from 1 p.m.-4 p.m.; it is free.

Down on Bristol's historic waterfront you'll find **Eliza's,** one of the best restaurants for many miles around. The building housing Eliza's, on the corner of State and Thames Streets, dates back to the 1800s. Then steamboats carrying passengers and freight docked at the wharves at the foot of State Street, and railroad cars rumbled by on Thames. The first floor of the building was originally a general store; the center stairway led to a boarding house above. Since the early 1800s, a succession of taverns and restaurants has inhabited the old structure; Eliza's was established in 1973 by Ed and Beth Gerrior.

Eliza's

ONE STATE STREET
BRISTOL, RHODE ISLAND
253–2777

Downstairs two small dining rooms hold about 20 tables and a pleasant bar. The atmosphere is one of warmth and quaint candlelit charm; red brick walls are highlighted with original paintings by local artists and a collection of old oak sideboards. Upstairs there is another attractive dining area, used mostly on weekends or for private parties. Floor-to-ceiling windows behind the upstairs bar offer a sweeping view of the waterfront beyond.

The best test of a small restaurant is the aroma from its kitchen, and Eliza's passes that test with flying colors! Even before you've tasted a bite, you know the meal will be memorable. House specialties include boneless stuffed breast of chicken baked in pastry with cranberry glaze, delectable shrimps scampi, and veal with mustard sauce. Everything on the menu is prepared with imagination and care, including the desserts created by Beth. Try her superb baklava or perhaps the spicy raisin and walnut pie, or (our choice) chocolate cheesecake with an apricot glaze.

If you can't arrange to be there for dinner, Eliza's luncheon menu—though not so varied—won't disappoint you. Excellent clam chowder and quiche are always available, plus salads, sandwiches, crepes and omelets, several entrees, and those luscious desserts.

Eliza's is located at One State Street, Bristol, RI (401) 253-2777. It is open for lunch Monday through Friday 11:30 a.m.-2:30 p.m., and for dinner Monday through Saturday 5 p.m.-10 p.m. Prices are moderate. Reservations are advisable for dinner. American Express, MasterCard, Visa, Diner's Club and Carte Blanche are accepted.

Southern Coastline to Westerly

Next, we'll head over across Narragansett Bay and drive down along the coast. From Newport, take Rte. 138 west and connect with Scenic Rte. 1A south just past the Jamestown Bridge. Rte. 1A more or less follows the coastline all the way to Point Judith. The small fishing village of **Galilee** is just a short jog to the west. Visitors may watch the fishing fleet unload the day's catch and buy seafood straight from the ocean to take home: fresh lobsters, quahogs, clams, and many varieties of fish. Each summer Galilee is the site of the Rhode Island Tuna Tournament Rodeo, followed by the Roger Williams Shark and Bluefish Tournament. For those not interested in fishing, there are ocean sight-seeing cruises, a cluster of attractive gift shops, and a marvelously long and sandy state beach.

To the west across Point Judith Pond (a tidal inlet) lies **Jerusalem,** sister village to Galilee. To get there, take Rte. 108 north to Rte. 1; follow Rte. 1 west and south to Succotash Road, and turn left. Jerusalem is a delight—tinier even than Galilee, it is also an authentic fishing community, unspoiled and un-touristy. Several more fine beaches are nearby.

Many people tend to think of coastal villages and beaches as summertime lures only, but we think they're just as appealing (sometimes more so) in winter. They are all yours then, for one thing—no crowds, no traffic jams. The Galilee and Jerusalem fishing fleets work year-round, some seafood restaurants stay open all year, and the empty stretches of beach are perfect for long, bracing walks. Bird watching is rewarding in winter, too; we spotted two swans in Snug Harbor, just north of Jerusalem.

From Jerusalem, take Rte. 1 west and then pick up Scenic 1A again at Haversham. The road meanders down to Watch Hill, a serene old summer resort town, and then goes north to Westerly. Here, we suggest a tour of **The Babcock-Smith House.** Built in the 1730s, the handsome old place is of Georgian architecture, with an extension in the rear that gives it the appearance of a saltbox. Dr. Joshua Babcock was the first physician in the area; later he was appointed postmaster by Benjamin Franklin, who often visited the house.

The historic Babcock-Smith House, at 124 Granite Street in Westerly, is open Sundays from 2-5 p.m. May through June and September through October, Sundays and Wednesdays in July and August, and by appointment at other times. Telephone (401)596-5704. Admission is $1.

At the Westerly Hospital, travelers may view an unusual item—**a cap that belonged to Florence Nightingale.** Displayed in a glass case, the lacy memento may be found at the rear of the hospital's lobby, next to the elevators. The cap, worn by Nightingale in the Crimea in 1854, was placed in the hospital in 1965 on the anniversary of the famed nurse's birth. In case you've forgotten the details, she went to the Crimean war front in an attempt to overcome the grossly unsanitary and inefficient conditions existing in British military hospitals of that day. And she succeeded: the death rate in those hospitals was reduced from 42% to 2% in only five months. If you would like a souvenir, postcards portraying Nightingale's cap are on sale in the hospital's gift shop.

Westerly has a very nice small park right in the center of town. **Wilcox Park** was designed by the Boston firm of Olmsted, founded by Frederick Law Olmsted, famed landscape architect and park planner of the late 1800s. On Broad Street, abutting the park, note the Memorial and Public Library. Gracing its front lawn is a bench. It is **Gladys Ormphby's "Trysting Bench,"** presented to the town by Ralph Edwards of "This Is Your Life" in honor of TV star Ruth Buzzi, a native of Westerly. Buzzi played the role of dowdy, hair-netted Gladys on "Laugh-In." Cast back in your memory and visualize the scene: Gladys is sitting on the bench. Arte Johnson, would-be masher and Dirty Old Man, sidles up and sits beside her. Gladys, indignant at his guttural mutterings, hits him with her purse; he topples over. End of scene. The "Trysting Bench," by the way, is on view only in summer. During the wintertime it is put away by park district personnel for preservation.

Wyoming/Arcadia

Not far from Westerly (about 15 miles northeast) the Wyoming/Arcadia region is typically New England "country"—farms and fields, woods, meandering brooks and narrow, curving roads. If you are coming from Westerly, take Rte. 3; from Newport, follow Rte. 138 west. The two routes cross at Wyoming, an 18th-century mill village.

Meadowbrook Herb Garden, on Rte. 138 about a mile east of the crossroads, sells herb plants, seeds, seasonings, and teas. Even if you don't know basil from bay leaves, stop in and look around. The delightfully fragrant shop offers a nice selection of gifts, very attractively displayed. In addition to all the herbal products, visitors will find linen tea towels, teapots, aprons, paintings, stained glass window ornaments, notepaper and table mats with herbal designs, and a number of books about herbs or cooking with herbs.

There are charming handcarved wooden toys, stuffed animals and hand puppets, too, plus rows of jams, jellies and honey, and a tempting array of imported cookies. A large picture window offers a splendid view of the formal garden out back. The greenhouse runs alongside, entered through a doorway in the shop. Walk down the steps and inhale as you go—the scent of growing herbs is something to savor. Like the shop, the greenhouse is neat as a pin and exceedingly pleasing to the eye. Here you may purchase a cutting or a plant to take home.

Meadowbrook's 11 acres produce more than 50 varieties of herbs; they are sold individually or in blends. The lengthy list includes seasoning herbs such as comfrey, sage, tarragon and dill, and tea herbs with romantic-sounding names like cowslip flowers, heart's ease, English daisy and lemonbalm. Potpourri mixtures are available, too, as are essential oils of anise, citronella, rosemary, eucalyptus, thyme, clove and many others, plus all manner of spices.

Heinz Grotzke, owner of Meadowbrook, has been an herb grower virtually all of his life. He came to this country from the Pomeranian region of Germany in 1955, and established Meadowbrook in 1966. An amiable, gentle man, Grotzke takes justifiable pride in the quality of his herbs. They are grown bio-dynamically, a method of agriculture based on the teachings of Rudolf Steiner.

Steiner, an Austrian philosopher at the turn of the century, generated far-reaching ideas in many fields—such as education, art, architecture and social organization. His emphasis was always on the fundamental interdependence of man and nature. Grotzke explains Steiner's approach: "It reaches beyond one's farm or garden to view our planet as a huge and complex organism of which the cultivated soil is but one living organ. Wherever a person holds responsibility for a parcel of land, his or her proper care *or* careless action will have a universal effect upon the entire earth organism through the soil."

In the production of herbs this means that the plants are not only grown organically but are then hand-selected both in the field and drying house, chopped by hand, carefully dried, hand-rubbed to remove all stems and finally packaged or stored under optimum conditions. The entire endeavor is one of complete commitment: "a totality comprised of bio-dynamic fertilization, cleanliness in growing, purity and know-how in processing, and appearance, fragrance, and excellence in packaging."

The result is a dried herb of a quality very different from—and far superior to—most commercial offerings. Considering all of the time and labor that go into creating the final product, Meadowbrook's prices are astonishingly low. And it's a fascinating place to visit. If you would like to know more about Rudolf Steiner's teachings, by the way, the shop has a number of his books for sale.

Meadowbrook Herb Garden is located on Rte. 138, Wyoming, RI 02898 (401)539-7603. It is open Tuesday to Friday from 10 a.m.-noon and 1-4:30 p.m., Saturday from 10 a.m.-noon and 1-4 p.m., Sunday 1-4 p.m. Closed holidays, from Christmas Eve to January 6, and on Monday (except during the spring months).

Back at the junction of Rtes. 3 and 138 in Wyoming, turn left on Rte. 3. Take the first right, then bear right again at the fork onto Old Nooseneck Hill Road. That will lead you deep into the woods (about three miles) to Summit Road, the hamlet of Arcadia, and **Dovecrest**, Rhode Island's only American Indian restaurant.

Ferris and Eleanor Dove, whose tribal names are Chief Roaring Bull and Princess Pretty Flower, have operated this unique establishment for 16 years. Situated in a white farm-house built in the late 1700s, Dovecrest has two dining areas: the comfortable, wood-paneled Indian Room and a sunny porch called the "Solarium." The latter's louvered windows make it a pleasant place to dine winter or summer, with a nice view of lawn, woods, and a tumbling brook. Downstairs there is a cocktail lounge, entered from the outside through a wooden "wigwam."

As is only proper for an authentic American Indian restaurant, Dovecrest's menu offers buffalo steak and buffalo pot pie. For less adventurous appetites there are steaks, chops, chicken, seafood and sandwiches. Succotash, made with kidney beans, creamed corn and onion, is available in season. Desserts include Indian pudding, plus homemade pies and cheesecake. But the Dovecrest specialty is an old Rhode Island favorite—small cornmeal patties called jonnycakes.

Originally known as "journey cakes," these patties were invented by the Indians as a tasty snack to pack along for lunch on the trail. The early white settlers copied the idea, but somewhere along the way the name became "jarney" and finally "jonny-cake," sometimes spelled "johnny-cake." The cakes are served piping hot with butter and maple syrup, with bacon or sausage on the side. A great deal of amicable controversy exists between various regions of the state as to which makes the best cakes, and recipes differ. The Dovecrest version is a mixture of homeground cornmeal, boiling water, salt and a smidgen of sugar, formed into patties and fried till nicely browned.

You may be wondering how an American Indian restaurant (or any restaurant for that matter) ever got started as far off the beaten path as Dovecrest is. Mrs. Dove, a charming, friendly woman, told us that she started out in the catering business. Then she opened a guest house here in tiny Arcadia Village. But her husband had once promised her that she would never have to get up in the mornings to cook breakfast—and suddenly she found herself doing just that, for her guests. "Why don't you open a restaurant instead, and serve only lunch and dinner?" her husband asked. So she did . . . and Dovecrest came into being.

Mr. and Mrs. Dove, both fullblooded descendants of the old Narragansett tribe, are very active in local Indian affairs. Mr. Dove, a council member of the present tribe, is also its war chief. (Back in the 1600s there were some 30,000 Narragansetts in southern New England; today there are only about 1000, 600 of them living in Rhode Island.) And Dovecrest is the site of a number of Indian events throughout the year, to which the public is invited. In June, for instance, a Strawberry Thanksgiving takes place. In July there is the Green Bean Thanksgiving and Clambake, in October cranberries are honored, and in November a Harvest Thanksgiving Dinner is held. At each event thanks are offered for the bounty of the seasonal harvest, and there is entertainment—Indian ceremonial dances, songs and storytelling.

In addition to the restaurant, Dovecrest has an Indian gift shop, **The Trading Post.** It's located in a separate building just across the yard. The Ferrises have assembled crafts from the major Indian tribes of North America—many are original, one-of-a-kind items. From the Southwest come copper and silver jewelry made by the Zunis and Navajos; there are Navajo cradle boards and Cree leather bags and headbands. Patchwork jackets and capes are made by the Seminoles of Florida's Everglades, handcarved primitive sculpture by the Eskimos, ivory and scrimshaw carvings by the Tlingit Indians.

There are moccasins and sweet grass baskets and beadwork handmade by several tribes, and distinctive pottery by Sara Ayer, last of the Catawba potters. Wood carvings and totem poles come from the Sioux of South Dakota and the Cherokees of North and South Carolina. Many locally made items are offered, too: exquisite beadwork created at the post by Princess Red Wing, watercolors by Diosa, leather crafts by Nas-Ta-Bega and Sun Woman, and a selection of fine silver jewelry by Toni Chin. Chin's silver feather necklaces and delicately wrought bracelets are especially noteworthy.

Dovecrest, Summit Road, Arcadia Village, Exeter, RI 02822, (401)539-7795, is open daily from 11:30 a.m.-9 p.m., year-round. Prices are moderate. The Trading Post is open Monday through Friday, 11 a.m.-8 p.m., Saturday and Sunday 11:30 a.m.-9 p.m. Telephone or write for information about the various Indian events and reservations for same.

Either before or after you visit Dovecrest, stop in at the **Tomaquag Indian Memorial Museum** right next door. Situated in a rustic old shingled building, the museum contains a fascinating collection of Indian artifacts from a bygone era. Indian dolls, pottery, rugs, baskets, jewelry, games, clothing and wampum are interestingly displayed. Also on view are Indian "scare faces," stuffed animals and birds, replicas of Indian boats, dioramas, and several private collections. But the most intriguing "exhibit" in the museum is its curator, Princess Red Wing.

The Princess, a delightful, witty and talented woman of 84, is a descendant of Philip, sachem of the Wampanoags. (He was the noted Indian chief who waged "King Philip's War" against his white neighbors in the late 1600s—with good reason, according to most historians.) Princess Red Wing is also squaw sachem of the New England Council of Chiefs, among several other impressive Indian titles. Her knowledge of Native American history, particularly that of the Indians of Southern New England, is vast, and she thoroughly enjoys sharing it.

Groups of schoolchildren come often to the museum, where the Princess regales them with Indian legends, teaches them a bit of Indian history, games and dances, and shows them something of the ancient crafts—crushing corn in a wooden mortar or weaving baskets, for example.

If the museum isn't open when you are in Arcadia, try the Dovecrest—Princess Red Wing may be there. Sometimes she plays the piano and sings Indian melodies, and on Monday and Wednesday afternoons she reads tea leaves. Red Wing most definitely is on hand for the various Indian ceremonies held regularly at Dovecrest. When you meet her, ask her to tell you about Tomaquag, the sleek, mounted beaver in the museum. "Tomaquag," by the way, *means* beaver. It is a long story, and a charming one. The beaver, presented to the Princess by the Smithsonian Institution a year ago, is freeze-dried!

Tomaquag Indian Memorial Museum, Summit Road, Arcadia Village, Exeter, RI 02822, is open daily from 11 a.m.-4 p.m., more or less. School and Scout groups are welcome by appointment; telephone Dovecrest, (401)539-7795.

Dovecrest and Tomaquag Indian Memorial Museum are only five minutes away from **Arcadia State Park and Management Area** with beautiful wooded drives, a bathing beach, boating and fishing.

Providence

Some travelers think of Rhode Island's capital only as an

industrial city, to be driven through as fast as possible in order to reach other regions of the state. If such a thought is floating around in your mind, dismiss it. Providence, founded by Roger Williams in 1636, holds a number of unexpected pleasures for visitors willing to leave the highway and explore.

On the East Side, the **College Hill Historic District** abounds with fine old houses, churches and other notable structures. The entire area, in fact, is a National Historic Landmark—the site of Colonial Providence. Brown University and the Rhode Island School of Design (the latter with an excellent art museum) are located within this district, too.

Across the river, right in the center of downtown Providence between Weybosset and Westminster Streets, you'll find the **Arcade.** A handsome Greek Revival building, this "temple of trade" was cited by the Metropolitan Museum as one of the finest remaining examples of 19th-century commercial architecture.

Indoors, three tiers of shops and cafes open onto long balconies, graced with the original cast-iron railings. Overhead, glass skylights are supported by wooden beams. Outdoors, both entrances are fronted by six massive Ionic columns, each 22 feet high and weighing more than 12 tons. (It took one worker 30 days to cut a single column, which was then transported from Graniteville, Rhode Island, to Providence by teams of oxen.)

If you examine both entrances to the Arcade, you will note that the facades don't match. That's because two different architects worked on the building: they agreed on the overall plan, but each was determined to design his own facade. The Westminster Street side, attributed to James Bucklin, has the familiar triangle of the Greek pediment. The Weybosset Street side, thought to be Russell Warren's contribution, has a series of stone panels.

Cyrus Butler, an enterprising gentleman, built the Arcade in 1828 as America's first indoor shopping mall. He was obviously a man well ahead of his time; skeptics of the day called the edifice "Butler's Folly" . . . a "foolhardy dream." But for almost a century and a half the Arcade carried out Butler's intent, housing a variety of merchants—and managing to survive a fire, three hurricane floodings, and, at one point, threatened demolition. Then, in the 1970s, neglect and lack of tenants turned the Arcade into little more than a walk-through from one street to another. The building seemed doomed.

In 1980, however, a Maryland development firm bought the structure and spent some $3,000,000 to renovate it, carefully preserving and restoring its 19th-century architectural splendors. Today, the 153-year-old "Great Lady" is once again proving Butler's detractors to be wrong. The Arcade is now a spacious, airily handsome setting for a colorful contemporary array of quality merchandise.

The lower level, called the "Street of Eateries," is lined with shops offering fine wines, cheese, candy, ice cream, freshly baked chocolate chip cookies, spices, gourmet foods and kitchenware, plus several small restaurants. The central court—reminiscent of a European street cafe—is dotted with umbrella-topped tables where shoppers may relax, eat, and observe the passing scene.

The "Shops of the Arcade," on the second level, feature a variety of fine clothing, accessories and gifts. The third level, "The Galleria," presents silks, porcelain and enamelware imported from China, Himalayan rugs and handiwork, art exhibits from the Rhode Island School of Design, and an attractive pub-restaurant.

In sum, the Arcade is fun—a magnificently-designed, historic structure once more alive with the sights, sounds and good smells of a thriving marketplace. Cyrus Butler would be pleased!

If you haven't indulged in too many snacks at the Arcade and want a really good lunch or dinner, we recommend **Pot au Feu**. The restaurant is only a two-minute walk away, to the left off Weybosset Street.

Located on two levels in the old Custom House, Rich and Jan Fensterer's Pot au Feu has a pleasantly relaxed ambiance. Downstairs, in the basement Bistro, the building's granite foundations are visible below walls of red brick and beamed ceilings. Wood-topped tables, each with a vase of fresh flowers, are inset with handsome old French tiles. The bar, just inside the lower entrance, is zinc-topped—another authentic French touch. The Salon, upstairs, is rather more elegant with white tablecloths, carpeting and a handsome chandelier. But it's not dauntingly formal, either.

The Bistro offers an appetizing selection of moderately-priced soups, quiches and omelets, salads, sandwiches and entrees, including several interesting daily specials. The last time we were there we sampled the cream of potato with Brussel sprouts soup, and an excellent salad called "Astoria": a melange of rice, apples, pecans and walnuts, raisins, celery, scallions, ginger root and chunks of ham and chicken.

"Le Menu" for the Salon is more extensive, and pricier: you may order a la carte or choose the prix fixe which includes everything from appetizer to dessert. Nine entrees are available, ranging from roast duckling with caramelized orange sauce to tournedos of beef, sauteed chicken breast in a nut sauce, or scallops of veal. For dessert, try the Mousse au Citron or Creme Caramel. Or, if you're feeling too well fed, practice a modicum of restraint with one of the restaurant's numerous coffees accompanied by a brandy from Pot au Feu's lengthy list.

Pot au Feu is located at 44 Custom House Street, Providence, (401)273-8953. The Bistro is open daily from 11:30 a.m.-10 p.m., on Friday and Saturday to midnight. The Salon is open Tuesday through Friday from 1:30 p.m.-9 p.m., on Saturday to 10 p.m., and reservations are advisable. Visa, MasterCard and American Express are accepted.

Those of you who appreciate zoos will be pleased to know that Providence has a good one. It is part of **Roger Williams Park;** the park's 450 hilly acres also include gardens, several ponds and lakes and the Park Museum of Natural History and Planetarium. The zoo offers a New England farmyard section, a Tropical American building and North American exhibits including polar bears, timber wolves, elk, bison, sea lions and—our favorite—a prairie dog village.

Roger Williams Park is on Elmwood Avenue about three miles south of downtown Providence. It is open daily except holidays from 10 a.m.-4 p.m.

Off the Beaten Path in Massachusetts

The North Shore

Most of the towns along Massachusetts' scenic coastline north of Boston are very well known indeed. There is Marblehead, with its narrow, winding streets and perfect little harbor. Gloucester is renowned for its picturesque fishing fleet, Rockport for its art colony and shops. Salem, to practically everyone, means witches. And then there is Beverly.

Situated just north of Salem across the Bass River, Beverly is basically an industrial town noted for shoe manufacturing. Back in the 1600s John Endecott, first governor of the Massachusetts Bay Colony, nicknamed the small settlement "Beggarly." Despite its detractors, the town managed to develop into a prosperous 18th-century seaport. And, in 1775, America's first naval vessel was built here—the schooner *Hannah*, commissioned by General George Washington.

Today, compared to some of its quaintly pretty neighbors, Beverly is not a star. On Sundays, however, the town offers visitors a unique treat. At 3:15 and again at 8 p.m., an elegantly restored old vaudeville theater on downtown Cabot Street comes to life with one of the most delightful performances imaginable. The show is called **Marco the Magi's Production of Le Grand David and His Own Spectacular Magic Company,** and it is best described by quoting the playbill:

> A Rhapsodical Spectacle Headed by Marco the Magi, Le Grand David and Seth the Sensational ... with Monsieur Le Professeur Enrico Besco, Mademoiselle Sonya, Edlita, a bevy of tap dancers, a barbershop chorus, Spanish clowns, assorted assistants both handsome and beautiful, cavorting creatures of every description, and virtuoso performers of piano, trumpet, trombone, accordion, flute, song and dance. Spellbinding! Dazzling! Opulent! Entertaining! Baffling! Fabulous!

Every one of these glowing adjectives is justified. Authorities have judged *Le Grand David* equal to the best of the troupes that toured the Americas and Europe during the

DAVIDSON COLLEGE LIBRARY
DAVIDSON, N. C.

39

19th century when the art of conjuring was at its height. The American Museum of Magic calls the production "The finest magic show in the world today." But the intriguing thing is that the 70-odd performers and technicians in the troupe are all talented amateurs, magic-loving local folk who come together each week to create an unforgettable, joyous presentation of amazing tricks and illusions.

Now in its fifth year, *Le Grand David* is the realization of a lifelong dream of its founder, Marco the Magi. In everyday

life Marco (an adept magician) is Cesareo Pelaez, a psychology professor at nearby Salem State College and a onetime student of the renowned humanist Abraham Maslow. Ever since he was a child in his native Cuba and saw the famed Fu Manchu traveling troupe, Pelaez had wanted to mount his own magic show—based on the old, classic traditions. After Castro's takeover, he fled from Cuba to the United States; in 1976 Pelaez and 17 other investors pooled $110,000 to buy Beverly's Cabot Street Theater as a showplace for their newly-formed production.

Le Grand David himself is handsome young David Bull, a Boston University psychology major when he met Pelaez. Seth the Sensational, now all of eight, began performing in the show when he was only four years old. The troupe also includes lawyers, housewives, architects, sales clerks, bankers and teachers. In addition to performing with contagious enthusiasm, they do everything from making the costumes and constructing the sets to selling candy, coffee and pastries during intermission.

The show actually begins out on the sidewalk, with the tuxedoed doorman offering a greeting and advice on where to park your car. Inside, you walk through the mouth of a great green "dragon" into the theater lobby where jugglers, clowns and puppeteers entertain waiting ticket holders. Then it's showtime. A friendly clown suggests you hurry; seats are not assigned and you don't want to be too far away from the stage. A gong sounds, deep and thrilling; the curtain flies up, and—amid a cloud of billowing smoke—the action begins!

Visually the production is extraordinary: the lavish backdrops and exquisite Oriental-style costumes are breathtaking. The swiftly paced 2½-hour program includes countless levitations, transformations, sleights of hand and miraculous escapes, interspersed with bits of charming buffoonery and rousing musical numbers. Performers are deftly sliced in half and then put back together again; rabbits and doves magically appear and disappear, as well as three raucously quacking ducks; there is even a waltzing "cow." The production ends with a smashing grand finale—and then the entire cast races out into the lobby to line up and bid you farewell.

Le Grand David is pure fun, for audience and actors alike. It's more than just a show; it is an experience of total immersion into the world of enchantment!

Marco the Magi's Production of Le Grand David and His Own Spectacular Magic Company is held at the Cabot Street Theater, 286 Cabot Street, Beverly, MA 01915 (617)927-3677. Follow Rte. 1A north from Salem over the bridge. Where 1A veers left, stay right and you are on Cabot Street. The theater is on the left a few blocks up. Performances are given on Sundays at 3 and 8:15 p.m. Around Christmas there may be extra shows, and for about six weeks each summer the cast takes a vacation, so please call ahead and check. Admission: adults $4.50, children under 12 and senior citizens $3; loge seats 50¢ additional. Tickets will be mailed to you if there is time enough; otherwise, you may pick them up at the door.

If you'd like to dine in Beverly before or after the show, there are two good restaurant choices available not far from the Cabot Street Theater. **The Beverly Depot,** the more elegant of the two, is situated in a restored 1897 railroad station. The main dining area, once the waiting room, has a handsome wooden beamed cathedral ceiling, soft lighting, and hanging plants. Brasses from locomotives, old railroad photos and other appropriate mementos decorate the adjoining comfortable lounge-bar. A nice touch when we were there was a pottery pitcher of fresh daisies on the bar itself. Beef and fish, in combinations or alone, are the Depot's specialties along with ratatouille, excellent baked potatoes and a salad bar. Prices are moderately expensive, ranging from about $6 to $15.

Ample parking is provided behind the restaurant and across the tracks. One word of caution: the Depot is on the main line of the Boston & Maine Railroad and trains still roll by regularly. So please look both ways before crossing the tracks!

To find the Beverly Depot, ask at the theater or return to the fork of Rte. 1A and Cabot Street and turn right on 1A for about two blocks. On the left, across a small park, you will see the Depot. Hours are from 5 p.m.-10 p.m. weekdays, and 5 p.m.-11 p.m. Sundays. Telephone: (617)927-5402.

Charlie Amore's Capri Restaurant, up the street from the theater, is a pleasantly casual, family-style establishment. The menu offers a fine selection of Italian entrees, but we recommend the enormous Sicilian-style pizzas—especially if you have youngsters along. The pizzas are so large that one could conceivably feed four people, at a very reasonable price.

The Capri Restaurant, at 139 Cabot Street, Beverly, (617) 922-9776, is open daily from 4 p.m.-11:30 p.m. Parking is available at the rear.

Salem, south over the bridge from Beverly, offers visitors a wealth of attractions. Its many historic structures include the 1642 Witch House and The House of the Seven Gables; Pickering Wharf has a cluster of interesting shops and restaurants. **The Peabody Museum** at 161 Essex Street, East India Square, was founded by sea captains and contains several fine maritime collections and an excellent gift shop. Highly recommended for dining is **The Lyceneum** at 43 Church Street; Sunday brunch here is renowned.

From Salem, Rte. 114 will take you to Marblehead. One of the most charming towns in New England, Marblehead is made for walking. In fact, you'd better explore on foot, at

Grandmother's. Natick, MA.

least the old section; the streets, many one way, are maddeningly confusing. Our favorite place to rest weary feet is **The Barnacle,** on Front Street at the harbor just before Fort Sewell. In good weather you may sit outside on the tiny deck and enjoy a bowl of clam chowder while watching boats and sea gulls. For a different view of the harbor and ocean, drive out to Marblehead Neck. Follow Atlantic Avenue (Rte. 129) south to Ocean Avenue and turn left. On your way back, follow Beach Street to Atlantic Avenue; at the corner you'll find **Stowaway Sweets,** a fine candy shop tucked away in a small, ivy-covered house surrounded by a lovely garden.

Evelyn and George Moore established Stowaway Sweets in 1929, and their candies have achieved international fame! For eleven years of President Franklin D. Roosevelt's administration, the White House ordered weekly shipments of their wares. Mrs. Calvin Coolidge was also a loyal customer, as were England's Queen Mary and Lady Astor. Stowaway Sweets' chocolates are hand-dipped and made fresh daily on the premises. The shop offers dark and milk chocolates with a multitude of cream, hard or chewy centers, almond butter crunch, chocolate-covered nuts and fruits, and fudge—and you may choose your own selection, a rare treat nowadays.

Stowaway Sweets is at 154 Atlantic Avenue, Marblehead, MA 01945 (617)631-0303. Open daily from 9 a.m.-5:30 p.m., Sundays from 11 a.m.-4 p.m. No credit cards are accepted, but personal checks are all right.

Gloucester is situated ten miles northeast of Salem and Beverly. Follow Rte. 127 north; at Magnolia (just south of Gloucester) pick up Shore Road. It will lead you to Hesperus Avenue, which connects again with 127 further north. Along the way you will come to **Hammond Castle Museum,** on the right. Even if it is not open when you're there, stop anyway; you may roam around the grounds and admire the marvelous view of the ocean beyond. The rocks you see are said to be the famed Norman's Woe, the reef immortalized in Longfellow's poem, "The Wreck of the Hesperus."

If Hammond Castle is open, please take time for a tour; it is a remarkable place. John Hays Hammond was an inventor, and an inveterate collector of medieval art. In 1928 he designed the castle—complete with drawbridge—to house his collection. The Great Hall, 100 feet long, 58 feet high and 25 feet wide, contains a magnificent pipe organ. Hammond (not related to the organ Hammonds) built the instrument himself. We are particularly enamored of the inner court-yard, walled by authentic medieval European facades. Tropical plants surround a large pool, into which Hammond was said to have dived from time to time from a balcony above. Best of all, the courtyard has its own weather system that can change from sunlight to a tropical downpour, then to romantic moonlight!

The Hammond Castle Museum is located at 80 Hesperus Avenue in Magnolia (a part of Gloucester). From April to November the Castle is open daily from 10 a.m.-4 p.m.; in December and from February to March, Tuesday to Friday 10 a.m.-3 p.m., Saturday and Sunday to 4 p.m. Closed Thanksgiving, Christmas and all of January. Admission: adults, $2.50; children under 13, $1.00. For further information, call (617)283-2080.

In Gloucester, a short side trip will bring you to another amazing structure, called **Beauport**. Drive past the town's famed Fish Pier and take a right on East Main Street. Past Rocky Neck, the road becomes Eastern Point Boulevard. Beauport will be on the right, the parking area on the left. (Note: Eastern Point Boulevard is a private road, open to visitors only when the museum is open.)

Beauport began as a small, shingled summer cottage built in 1904 by Henry Davis Sleeper, a Boston architect and interior designer. Sleeper wanted to create a house in which each room would reflect some aspect or period of American life. Little by little he added rooms, each one organized around some outstanding (sometimes bizarre) object or collection of objects such as a Federal doorway, a set of carved wooden hearse windows, Lord Byron's bed, and an iron stove in the form of George Washington. Eventually Sleeper's fertile imagination and decorating instincts culminated in a mansion of some 40 rooms, all different as to light, color, shape, texture and style.

Many notable guests visited Beauport during its owner's lifetime, including Eleanor Roosevelt, John Marquand, Eugene O'Neill, Noel Coward and Henry James. Sleeper died in 1934; today Beauport belongs to The Society For the Preservation of New England Antiquities.

Beauport, on Eastern Point Boulevard in Gloucester, MA, is open Monday to Friday from 10 a.m.-4 p.m. May 15 to mid-September. From mid-September through October 31, it is open only on weekends from 1 p.m.-4 p.m.; closed rest of year. Adults (13 and over) $3, children 6 to 12 $1.50, under 6 free. For further information call (617)227-3956.

Rockport lies further out along Cape Ann; just beyond the town there is a super spot for a picnic—**Halibut Point Reservation.** The Point is reached via a ten-minute walk through tangly, thicketed woods; in late July or early August huge, juicy blackberries may be picked along the way if you are willing to get off the path and don't mind suffering some wicked scratches from the prickly vines. You will also pass an old house, dating to the late 1600s. Halibut Point, a tumbled mass of huge rocks constantly battered by crashing surf, very much resembles the coast of Maine. You'll note old quarrying cuts on some of the rocks; in the early 1800s there were many granite quarries in this area.

One of the nicest things about Halibut Point is that it is not usually littered with people. Fishermen may sometimes be seen casting for whatever is running, but more often than not you will have the place pretty much to yourself. If you want to really be alone, come when the fog is in. Then the Point becomes a mysterious world of swirling mist, soundless except for the muffled boom of the ocean and the cries of invisible sea gulls.

To find Halibut Point Reservation, follow Rte. 127 (Granite Street) out of Rockport for about two miles; past Pigeon Cove watch for Gott Avenue on the right. There may or may not be a sign for Halibut Point; if you think you've gone too far, ask directions. The Reservation is open daily from sunrise to sunset; in summer there is a small parking fee.

Before leaving the Rockport area, you might be interested in a visit to the curious **Paper House.** The small structure—and all the furniture within—are made of specially treated, rolled newspapers! Why anyone would want to create a newspaper house is beyond us, but the Stenman family (who spent more than 20 years at it, beginning in 1922) was apparently fulfilling an artistic need. Supposedly, all of the newspapers can be unrolled and, if they were, would be in perfect, readable condition, now matter how old.

The Paper House, on Pigeon Hill Street in Rockport, is open daily from 10 a.m.-5 p.m., and there is a small admission fee.

The Boston Area

Most visitors to Boston spend their time exploring the city's multitude of historic sites: Paul Revere's House, the fascinating recycled waterfront and Faneuil Hall Market, and the like. There is, however, another Boston—a city of ordinary neighborhoods and ordinary people. If you'd like to capture the flavor of "the other Boston," try **Revere Beach,** especially in midsummer.

Just north of the city, Revere Beach is a lengthy expanse of sand and gentle surf, with a somewhat seedy air reminiscent of a faded Coney Island. "Proper Bostonians" do not come here; their summer habitats range from the upper reaches of the North Shore to Maine. But other local residents do flock to Revere Beach in large numbers; it could be called the Bar Harbor of triple-decker Boston. Even in wintertime the beach is not completely deserted. It's a fine place for a long, brisk walk if you don't mind being exposed to the elements.

Whenever you choose to be there, or even if you're just passing through, stop at **Kelly's** for a snack. The place looks pretty much like any other large seaside food stand, but the fare is far better than most. The roast beef sandwiches, in fact, are renowned. The people at Kelly's say they are world famous and they may well be! We particularly recommend the clam chowder—it's exceptional. The hot dogs, too, are great. Seafood, onion rings and other similar offerings are also available.

You will find Kelly's at 410 Boulevard, toward the north end of Revere Beach. Look for the brick-front building with the white roof and green sign with a shamrock. The connecting street (unmarked) is Oak Island.

South Boston is another neighborhood virtually ignored by travelers. Intensely Irish (it's where Boston's St. Patrick's Day Parade is held each year), the area has gained a reputation for being hostile to outsiders. We had heard of a restaurant there, however, that supposedly offered great food and a pleasantly old-fashioned atmosphere. So with a certain amount of trepidation, we fared forth one evening and headed for the wilds of "Southie"—to **Amrheins.**

Arriving unharmed and unaccosted, we discovered the restaurant to be exactly as described. Unpretentious, comfortable and obviously very popular, it was packed with local residents enjoying a night out. We chose to sit at a table in the bar, down a few steps from the main dining room. From our booth we could see—displayed in a case behind the ornately handcarved bar itself—Boston's first beer pump, dating back to the days when beer was pumped by steam.

As "Amrheins" is not an Irish name, we asked about its history. Charles Gilbert, who acts as host several nights a week, told us that the original owner was Bavarian. And the place, established in 1894, was originally an inn; railroad men, who made up most of the clientele, stayed in rooms upstairs when they were in town. Downstairs was a large bar that served food, much like Boston's venerable Jacob Wirth's. The menu in the old days was German. Gilbert remembers his father going to Amrheins for bratwurst and beer.

Today the restaurant, under new ownership since 1966, still offers a few German/Bavarian dishes, but basically the food is American with an Italian addition or two. Seven or eight specials are on each day; we chose smothered beef and liver and onions. The efficient, no-nonsense waitress quickly brought us each a loaded platter, and it was soon evident that Amrheins' fare was indeed excellent. Not fancy—just plain good food, at *very* reasonable prices. Mr. Gilbert explained that they suit the menu to the pocketbooks of the neighborhood: that a customer there can come in and have a good dinner five nights a week and not end up in the poorhouse.

We were mildly disappointed by the restaurant's desserts. The pie we ordered was only passable; other selections may be better and we will try again another time. In any case, Amrheins was definitely worth the trip. As for the purported animosity towards strangers, we felt none of it. After dinner we drove all around the area, exploring, and can report nary a sign of shillelagh violence towards us or anyone else in sight!

Amrheins is located at 80 W. Broadway, South Boston, MA; (617)268-6189. From downtown Boston follow Tremont Street south over the Massachusetts Turnpike; turn left on Herald Street and go three long blocks to the Broadway Bridge. Amrheins is one block beyond the bridge, on the left at the corner of W. Broadway and A Street. The restaurant is open daily from 11 a.m.; the kitchen closes at 9:45 p.m. The bar stays open generally until the last customer leaves. No credit cards are accepted: "We pay cash, you pay cash. We don't owe anybody!" Reservations are necessary only for large groups; otherwise it's first come, first served. Amrheins has its own parking lot, right next door.

48

Now, for a change of pace, we'll head over into Boston itself—to Boston proper and the epitome of Proper Boston—**Beacon Hill.** On Mount Vernon Street just below the historic Louisburg Square, there is a very appealing dining establishment called **Another Season.**

Chef-owners Odette Bery and Barbara Beckham took over the place (originally Au Beauchamp restaurant) about 2½ years ago. They restored the lovely turn-of-the-century French murals on the walls and set about creating their own atmosphere of quiet elegance and charm. The menu at Another Season is more or less Continental, featuring fresh foods that complement the seasons and including adaptations of dishes from many cuisines.

As the bill of fare changes weekly, we won't describe any particular item. We think you'll find whatever these two imaginative chefs suggest will be superb. There will be several soups and appetizers from which to choose, a selection of fish, meat and poultry dishes, one or two specials and, always, a vegetarian dish. The desserts vary from such inventive sweets as an almond chocolate cooky creation and walnut roulade with sour apple-cream filling to a simple pairing of fresh fruit and cheese. Another Season's wine list is excellent. Entree prices range from $7.50 to $12.

Another Season is at 97 Mount Vernon Street on Boston's Beacon Hill, one block off Charles Street. Open Monday through Thursday from 5:30 p.m.-10:30 p.m., Friday and Saturday from 5:30 p.m.-11 p.m.; closed Sundays. Reservations are advised; call (617)367-0880. American Express and MasterCard are accepted.

We've mentioned Proper Bostonians a time or two; at this point we would like to tell you about **Mt. Auburn Cemetery,** where the P.B.'s go when they depart this life (on their way to The Great Beacon Hill in the Sky).

Of all Proper Bostonian institutions, Mt. Auburn may well be the most select. Its roster of interments, called "The Roll of Distinction," includes such notables as Henry Wadsworth Longfellow, Amy Lowell, Oliver Wendell Holmes, several Cabots, Fannie Farmer (of cookbook fame), Isabella Stewart Gardner, Nathan Hale, Mary Baker Eddy and Winslow Homer. So traditional (and so important) is it for uppercrust Bostonians to be buried here that a poem concerning the place written around the turn of the century is still being reprinted today.

"A True Bostonian" tells the tale of a gentleman facing St. Peter at Heaven's Gate. "Sir," he is asked, "What claims do you present/To us to be admitted here?" The Boston Brahmin proudly lists his credentials: Boston born and bred, with honors from Harvard graduated, a pew in Trinity Church, and a villa in Nahant. "And last a handsome burial lot/In dead Mount Auburn's hallowed shades."

The verse ends: "St. Peter mused, and shook his head/Then as a gentle sigh he drew,/'Go back to Boston, friend,' he said,/'Heaven isn't good enough for you'."

Founded in 1831, Mt. Auburn was America's first garden cemetery. In those days this section of Cambridge was considered "out in the country" and had long been a rural retreat for Harvard students. Set up originally under the auspices of the Massachusetts Horticultural Society, the cemetery has from the first been famed for its magnificent collection of trees and flowering shrubs. Most of the trees are labeled with their common and scientific names and origins. At the gatehouse visitors may pick up a list of 100 of the most unusual specimens, with their locations. Also available are a booklet listing the names, occupations, dates of birth and death and plot numbers of almost 600 famous persons buried in Mt. Auburn Cemetery and a separate map indicating the locations of the graves of 55 notables.

Lest you think that tramping around a cemetery is a morbid pastime, we hasten to add that Mt. Auburn is remarkably beautiful! Its more than 170 hilly acres include some ten miles of winding roads, plus numerous paths and several lakes and ponds. The roadways and paths all have lovely names, too, mostly of flowers: Acacia, Marigold, Hyacinth, Dogwood, Cyclamen, Snowflake, and the like. From the tower high atop Mountain Avenue, there's a smashing view of the Boston skyline. In the spring, when the flowering shrubs are at their best, Mt. Auburn is absolutely breathtaking.

A proper demeanor, of course, is required from visitors. As the proprietors point out, it is a cemetery, not a public park. Not allowed, for example, are lolling about on the grass, sunbathing, bicycles, picnicking, dogs, or unaccompanied children under 14. Boisterous or undignified behavior will not be tolerated; blossoms, flowers and foliage must never be picked or disturbed. All of these restrictions aside (and they are certainly reasonable), Mt. Auburn is a marvelous place to explore. In addition to its scenic and horticultural appeal and list of greats, there are the monuments—sculptured illustrations of the Victorian passion for melancholy moral messages. Bird watchers love Mt. Auburn, too.

You will find the gates to Mt. Auburn Cemetery at 580 Mount Auburn Street, Cambridge, MA. Summertime hours are from 8 a.m.-7 p.m., wintertime hours 8 a.m.-sunset.

About four blocks from Mt. Auburn Cemetery, there is an interestingly different bakery where you can buy a lamejun. In case you don't know what that is, let us assure you that we didn't either before we went there. Now we know, and have become addicted. A lamejun, an Armenian specialty, is a meat pastry made with a mixture of lamb, beef, tomato, parsley and spices spread on dough and baked. The dough itself may be plain or garlic-flavored.

The Eastern Lamejun Bakery in Belmont is a marvelously zesty-smelling shop, redolent with the scents of herbs, spices and other good things. Besides lamejuns, you may also purchase meat, spinach or cheese turnovers, paklava (Armenian baklava), stuffed grape leaves, hommos, homemade sausages, and many other Middle Eastern delicacies. If you look into the back room, you will see a number of elderly women busily turning out the lamejuns and other items in vast numbers. Then wander around the store—there are spices (in bulk and otherwise), nuts of all kinds, filo dough, olives from Greece and Morocco, dried fruits, dried beans and chick peas, imported cheese, starter ingredients for yogurt, Syrian water pipes, kitchenware, and ordinary stuff like butter, milk and ice cream.

The bakery was established in 1941 by Charles and Mary Koundakjian, who had earlier fled their native Armenia to escape Turkish oppression. At first, Koundakjian's plan to open a shop to sell Armenian foods was looked upon with astonishment by his friends. "Who would buy a lamejun?" they wondered. Since then, the bakery's quarters have been enlarged three times, and countless lamejuns have come forth from the huge ovens to feed hungry customers. Word of the shop and its offerings has spread far afield; its name has even crept into modern fiction. Robert B. Parker, author of the Spenser detective series (and a regular patron) mentions Eastern Lamejun Bakery in his book, *Looking For Rachel Wallace*.

While we were there, we had a lengthy chat with Robert

Koundakjian, manager of the bakery since his parents' retirement. A delightfully enthusiastic, friendly man, he regaled us with tales of the shop's history and its continuing involvement with the Armenian community. Sadly, since our visit, Robert Koundakjian unexpectedly died. The shop will carry on, however, run by the family as always—in particular by Robert's brother Richard and son David.

The Eastern Lamejun Bakery, at 145 Belmont Street, Belmont, MA (617)484-5239, is open Monday through Saturday from 8 a.m.-6 p.m. If you're coming from Harvard Square, it is about a five-minute drive out Mt. Auburn Street toward Belmont; veer to the right just after the Star Market.

West of Boston
Waban/Newton Upper Falls/Wellesley

The Massachusetts Turnpike, known familiarly as the MassPike, is the fastest way of getting out of Boston. Some travelers, driven to the point of desperation by Boston's perplexing street system, look upon the Pike (a toll road) as a form of salvation. There are, however, other ways to head west. Rte. 9 is one, but we suggest that you try Beacon Street as an interesting alternative. It starts on Beacon Hill, wends its way through the city, then passes Chestnut Hill and Newton Center and ends in Waban, about 10 miles from Boston.

Just before you reach Waban Square, take a left onto Chestnut Street at the stoplight next to St. Philip Neri Church. Follow Chestnut, crossing under Rte. 9, to Newton Upper Falls. At the junction of Chestnut and Ellis Streets, you will find a cluster of old buildings—now designated an historic site. Scattered about in this small area are close to twenty antique shops, a veritable treasure trove for browsers. The shops' offerings are pleasingly varied—from oak and pine furniture to clocks, Orientalia, wicker, brass, jewelry and bric-a-brac. Hours vary, too, but visitors can generally count on a goodly number being open. One shop, called **Marcia and Bea,** is open daily from 10 a.m.-5 p.m., Sundays from 1 p.m.-5 p.m. Look for the sign; Marcia and her mother Bea may be found at 1009 Chestnut Street, around in back.

Two of the antique shops are located in the Mall on Elliot Street, a handsomely recycled mill complex on the bank of the Charles River. Tucked away at the rear of the courtyard is the entrance to **The Mill Falls Restaurant.** From the dining room and especially from the very comfortable cocktail lounge, there are marvelous views of the river, the falls, wooded hillsides and the graceful arch of Echo Bridge. In summertime, lunch and dinner are served outdoors on the restaurant's terrace.

The Mill Falls Restaurant is located at 383 Elliot Street, Newton Upper Falls, MA (617)244-3080. It is open for lunch Monday through Friday from 11:45 a.m.-2:30 p.m., for dinner Monday through Thursday from 5:30 p.m.-10 p.m., on Friday and Saturday to 11 p.m.; closed on Sunday. The cocktail lounge is open weekdays from 11:30 a.m.-2 a.m., Saturdays from 5:30 p.m.-2 a.m. Reservations are advised for lunch or dinner. A Continental cuisine is offered, and prices are fairly steep. All major credit cards are accepted.

Long ago, Indians built fish and eel weirs at this site above the falls; they dried the fish on the rocks on the opposite shore. A grist mill was erected here in 1688. Later a snuff business, the largest in New England, was added and in the late 1800s the complex became America's first silk mill. Silkworm cocoons by the millions were spun into silk, silk yarns and embroidery silks. The Mill Falls Restaurant was established in a portion of the complex in 1964.

Historic **Echo Bridge** and **Hemlock Gorge** may be reached by following Ellis Street a short distance up the hill. The bridge, completed in 1877, was built to carry the Sudbury River conduit across the Charles River. A triple stone arch, its foundations are sunk into solid rock. Climb down the steps beside the bridge. If you yell or even whisper from the bottom of the arch, a fine echo will respond—up to 18 times! We find that a maniacal laugh gets the best results.

The bridge is popular today with rope climbers, but we suggest you walk up and over. There's an excellent view of the falls and gorge from on top; on the other side you'll find several pleasant paths through the woods.

Next, follow Ellis Street down the hill and under Rte. 9 to Quinobequin Road in Waban. *Quinobequin* was the Indian name for the Charles River; it meant "clear water that twists and turns." At the end of the road, which follows along the river for about two miles, is **The Pillar House,** an 1828 mansion now a restaurant. The classic structure was built by Allen Crocker Curtis, whose father Solomon established one of the first paper mills in America. The large stone mill, built in 1834, still stands across the river. The Pillar House offers four dining rooms on two floors, and an upstairs cocktail lounge. The ambiance, appropriate for the lovely old house, is elegant.

The Pillar House, 26 Quinobequin Road, Newton Lower Falls, is open for lunch and dinner Monday through Friday; closed on weekends and for two weeks in July. Prices range from moderate at lunch to expensive for dinner; major credit cards are accepted. Hours are from 11:30 a.m.-9 p.m., to 10 p.m. on Fridays. Reservations are suggested: call (617) 969-6500.

A left at the light onto Washington Street (Rte. 16) will lead you to Wellesley Hills—about 3 miles. When you see the Babson College sign at Abbott Street, turn left and follow the road to the end. Then go left on Forest Street; turn in at the college's main gate. Watch for the signs directing visitors to the **Babson World Globe,** behind Coleman Hall. You will know when you've found it—it's enormous! The gigantic globe, 28 feet in diameter and weighing 25 tons, rotates on a 6-ton axis. A semicircle of benches offers a place to sit and watch.

The attractive town of Wellesley, just beyond Wellesley Hills on Rte. 16, is the home of Wellesley College. Both the main street and those leading from it are lined with posh shops of every kind. Afternoon tea (as well as other meals) is available at the **Treadway Wellesley Inn,** a charming old Colonial structure on Washington Street.

Just past the post office on the main street, take Crest Road over the railroad bridge and veer right on Linden Street to a small shopping center on the righthand side. Look for **The Cooky Jar,** approximately in the middle. This splendid bakery offers a great variety of delectable wares including honey graham bread, petit fours, rum cake and other Italian pastries, crisply thin cookies of all kinds, and a particularly luscious peach chocolate whipped cream cake.

The Cooky Jar is located at 173 Linden Street, Wellesley, (617)235-3196. It is open daily from 7:30 a.m.-6 p.m., Sundays from 7:30 a.m.-1 p.m.

Natick/Framingham/Marlboro

Now follow Washington Street (Rte. 16) southwest out of Wellesley to the rear entrance of **Wellesley College.** Take a drive around the campus and then proceed along Rte. 16, a winding road offering some nice views of the rambling

Charles River once again. After about 4½ miles you will see a sign for Natick; go right and connect with Rte. 27; it leads into Natick Center.

Casey's Diner in Natick is famous for great hot dogs. To get there, stay on Rte. 27 (Main Street) past the intersection with Rte. 135 (Central Street) and take the second right, South Avenue. Casey's will be on the left about three blocks down. The tiny building (only 8 feet by 24 feet with ten stools and a take-out window) has been designated a state landmark. Enter through the sliding door; the interior is all oak, including a well-scrubbed, somewhat elbow-dented counter. The Casey family has been in the hot dog vending business since 1885, starting with a horse-drawn lunch wagon. The present establishment, still family-operated, dates back to 1925. Don't miss all the old photos on the walls and the handsome copper bun steamer.

A nice touch: ladies are served their frankfurters cut into halves, for easier handling. The coffee, always freshly brewed, is excellent. The place is almost constantly jammed, and you may have to wait awhile for a seat. Enjoy: everyone in Casey's—owners and customers alike—seems to wear a friendly smile.

Casey's, 32 South Avenue, Natick, MA, is open Monday through Friday from 11:30 a.m.-9 p.m., Saturday from 11:30 a.m.-3 p.m.; closed on Sunday.

Back on Main Street (Rte. 27) follow along over the bridge; a short distance further on the left at No. 58 is a large building with the sign, **Grandmother's Mincemeat.** Back in 1899, Harrison L. Whipple (the present owner's great-grandfather) began making mincemeat in the back of his grocery store in downtown Natick, using *his* grandmother's recipe. Around 1910, the business grew too large for its quarters and Lewis Whipple, Harrison's son, began producing the mincemeat on a grander scale in a Natick factory. As mincemeat is seasonal, jams and jellies were added to the company's output and eventually other food items like pie fillings, bakers' jellies, fruit syrups and relishes. The Whipple Company moved into its present quarters, an old shoe factory, in 1947. Dight W. Crane (his mother was a Whipple) has been running it since 1970 and the firm now makes around 175 different products.

Inside, on each side of the front door, are narrow shelves holding samples of the company's wares. Anyone who stops in before 3 p.m. Monday through Friday may purchase a jar of Grandmother's Mincemeat (which is excellent), or marmalade, preserves, corn relish and the like from one of the friendly ladies in the office.

For anyone interested in fabrics, **Natick Mills** next door is a real find. Two floors covering an enormous expanse of space offer a fabulous assortment of drapery, upholstery, slipcover and dress fabrics. The pleasant clerks will help you make a selection, or will order anything you like from a wide variety of sources. Natick Mills also makes draperies, bedspreads and slipcovers, and does upholstering.

Located at 64 N. Main Street, Natick, MA, Natick Mills is open Monday, Tuesday and Saturday from 9 a.m.-5 p.m., Wednesday through Friday from 9 a.m.-9 p.m.; (617) 653-6550. The building also houses an antique warehouse and a children's clothing outlet.

From Natick, follow Rte. 135 to Framingham. A 19th-century book about Massachusetts called this old town, first settled in 1650, "the last outpost of civilization." Certain of the authors' acquaintances sniff at this description, declaring that the borderline lies much further east. Admittedly, Framingham's downtown area is not noted for its beauty, but trust us—we'll introduce you to some pleasant surprises.

From Rte. 135, take Rte. 126 to the right; veer left at the Memorial Building (Town Hall) onto Union Avenue and go left on Proctor Street. At the corner of Proctor and Franklin Streets, watch for the house with a giant candy cane out front. Inside the house, in a tiny room with a bow window, is **Barron's Candies.** Mr. Thomas Barron has been making his delicious confections, all by hand, for more than 50 years, and their quality is unmatched. We especially recommend the caramels, vanilla or fudge with or without nuts, and (in season) the old-fashioned hard candies called "peach blossoms." There are also chocolate-filled "chicken bones," all kinds of nut crunches and nut chocolate barks, hard candies in a wide assortment of flavors and much more. At holiday times the shop takes on a particularly festive air with brightly-wrapped candies appropriate to the season.

Barron's Homemade Candies is located at 81 Franklin Street, Framingham, (617)875-3725. Hours are Monday through Saturday from 10 a.m.-5:30 p.m., from 9:30 a.m. during holiday seasons; closed Sunday.

The Danforth Museum, a small but growing museum of

art that is worth a visit, is just around the corner on Union Avenue. In addition to changing exhibits, the Danforth's permanent collections include some fine 19th-century paintings and contemporary prints and sculpture. The children's room is fun for kids, with interesting color exhibits and a "do-it-yourself" portrait game. Youngsters (or adults) sit on a bench before a framed mirror and try on a wondrous selection of hats.

Housed in a recycled high school, the museum opened in 1975. Thomas Danforth, for whom it is named, held the original land grant that comprised Framingham and nearby towns—an area known as Danforth Farms. Danforth's family originally came from Framlingham, England. (That is not a typographical error: the spelling—and pronunciation—were changed somewhere along the way.)

The Danforth Museum, at 123 Union Avenue in Framingham, is open Wednesday through Sunday from 1-4:30 p.m.; closed on Christmas, New Year's Day, Thanksgiving and July 4. Admission is free.

From the Danforth, continue on Union Street to Rte. 9 and go west 8/10ths of a mile to the traffic light at Temple Street. Bear left on Temple to Salem End Road and turn right. About 6/10ths of a mile further you'll see a walled estate on your left, and the sign **Macomber Farm and Education Center.**

The late John E. Macomber, banker and philanthropist, left the property, a 46-acre pastoral site, to the Massachusetts Society for the Prevention of Cruelty to Animals. The Society opened the $7 million dollar farm and education center in May, 1981, and it is a unique venture. Some 100 horses, dairy and beef cattle, sheep, goats, pigs, turkeys and chickens live on the grounds. There are eight barns, a solar-heated reception center, and a pond for ducks, geese and swans. Devices throughout allow visitors to "feel" what horsepower means, see the world the way animals do (through special lenses), and understand how some animals walk by following marked wooden ramps.

In the barns are computer terminals programmed to provide information on the various animals, at different levels of interest, and a wealth of splendid graphics including huge color photographs. Visitors are invited to watch cows being milked, horses groomed and shod, and sheep being sheared. The animals may be petted, but only if they feel like it! The

57

Pillar House. Newton Lower Falls, MA.

idea of the center is not to provide a "petting zoo," but to teach people about farm animals in an entertaining way. Several picnic areas with benches and tables are available on the grounds, one of them beside a pretty pond surrounded by woods.

The Macomber Farm and Education Center is located at 450 Salem End Road, Framingham. Hours are from 10 a.m.-4 p.m.; closed in winter. Currently the center welcomes visitors daily in season, but because of zoning difficulties with the town it may have to close on weekends. If you wish to check, phone (617)879-5345. Macomber Farm is a fine place for a family outing, except for the prices which are a bit steep: $5 for adults, $2.50 for children.

Framingham Centre, just off Rte. 9 at Edgell Road, is the oldest section of the town. From Temple Street take Rte. 9 east to the off-ramp marked Edgell Road and bear left over the overpass. You will see the large common on your left, surrounded by churches and several other fine old structures. Julia Ward Howe's "Battle Hymn of the Republic" was first sung at Plymouth Church, to the right on Edgell Road.

Bear left on Vernon Street at the First Parish Unitarian Church; the small stone **Historical Society Building,** once a schoolhouse, is on the other side of the common at the corner of Grove and Vernon Streets. Constructed in 1837 of stone from a quarry on Salem End Road, the building replaced an earlier one on the same site, a brick schoolhouse erected in 1792. The Framingham Historical and Natural History Society keeps odd hours—from 2 p.m.-4 p.m., second and fourth Sundays, May through September—so you will have to plan ahead if you want to see the inside. (For research purposes, the building is also open Saturdays from 10 a.m.-noon). Permanent exhibits include antique furniture in a Victorian parlor, an early schoolroom, old portraits, farm tools and other memorabilia.

Wallace Nutting, author of numerous books on New England, lived in Framingham. His house stood on the site of the present-day Unitarian Church, and his furniture factory was located in downtown Framingham. An earlier resident of the town was Crispus Attucks, the black patriot and former slave who died in 1770 in the Boston Massacre.

Now follow Grove Street for three miles to Edmands Road and bear left; the unusually scenic drive will take you past lovely old houses (including two dating to the 1600s), farms, woods and open fields. If you follow it all the way, you'll come out in Marlboro. We usually turn off earlier, taking a right on Nixon Road. In season, **Hanson's Farm** on the left up the hill has the best fresh corn for miles around. Continuing on Nixon Road, veering to the left at Parmenter Road onto Hager Street, you will come to Rte. 20 and the back road to **The Wayside Inn** (of Longfellow fame) in Sudbury. Just to the left of the junction of Hager Street and Rte. 20 is the popular **Wayside Inn Country Store.**

Framingham has yet another surprise for visitors: **The Will C. Curtis Garden In the Woods.** To reach it, follow Edgell Road from Rte. 9 for two miles; at the stoplight at Water Street turn right, then take Hemenway Road to the left and follow the signs for the Garden. The way leads through an uninspiring suburban development, then rounds a bend and—suddenly—you find yourself deep in a forest!

An enchanting oasis in this solidly settled area, the Garden In the Woods is an outstandingly beautiful 45-acre woodland sanctuary. Some 2500 species and varieties of wild flowers and plants grow here in natural surroundings, the largest collection in the Northeast. Wear comfortable shoes and be prepared to hike; there are several miles of meandering trails. A map is available at the Nature Center near the entrance.

The garden's habitats range from forested high ground ridges to glacial kettle holes, ponds and streams, meadows, and lowland bog areas. There is a handsomely landscaped rock garden, too. Peak flowering season (with lady slippers, violets and scores of other delicate springtime blossoms) is from late April to June. In midsummer and early fall later-blooming wild flowers appear; sharp-eyed visitors may also spot frogs and turtles sunning themselves in lily pond and marsh.

Will C. Curtis, a naturalistic landscape gardener, began The Garden In the Woods in 1930. He and his lifelong friend and partner, Howard O. Stiles, developed the site over the years; in 1965 they turned it over to The New England Wild Flower Society. Now the Society's headquarters, the garden's Nature Center holds a 1500-volume library on native plants, gardening, landscaping and botany. For those interested, courses and field trips sponsored by the society are available.

The Garden In the Woods, Hemenway Road, Framingham, is open to the public from April 1 through October 31, Monday through Saturday from 8:30 a.m.-4:30 p.m.; closed Sunday. Admission is $1 for adults, children 50¢. For further information call (617)877-6574.

A good (and very inexpensive) place to eat in Framingham is **The Aegean,** a Greek restaurant that opened in early 1981 and is rapidly becoming locally popular. It is a comfortable small place with booths and widely spaced tables. The service is friendly, and the food is authentically Greek with some American dishes included on the menu as well. We enjoyed the house special platter, a sampling of sausages, meatballs, spinach pie, stuffed grape leaves, feta cheese, Greek olives and the like. The Aegean offers an unusual gyros dish, not sliced from the rack but formed into a spicy lamb and beef sausage served with raw onion on pita bread. Souvlaki (either beef or lamb), shishkabab, pastitsio and moussaka are also on the menu. Desserts include galactabouriko, baklava, rice pudding and pies. The restaurant hopes to acquire a limited liquor license in the near future so that wine and beer may be served.

The Aegean is located at 47 Beacon St., Framingham, MA; (617)879-8424. Getting there is a bit complicated: from Framingham Centre take Rte. 9 east 1½ miles to Rte. 126. Don't take the first 126 exit; go under the overpass and make a sharp right turn; follow the road up and around to the right and continue over the overpass to the intersection with Rte. 30. Turn left on 30 (which is also Beacon Street) and then left again at Kentucky Fried Chicken. The Aegean is in the mall down behind. You'll see the sign. Hours are from 8 a.m.-10 p.m. daily.

Over in Marlboro, there is another restaurant much favored by the authors, called **Keepers II.** Keepers II is situated on Fort Meadow Reservoir; the town dump is on the other side of the road, but fortunately the restaurant's windows face the water!

Keepers' decor, which changes from time to time, is always great fun and very colorful with contemporary graphics at their most imaginative. When we last visited, a Boston artist's silk prints adorned the light pine walls. Just inside the door was a clever display composed of a five-foot-tall artist's paintbrush and a pyramid of silvery paint cans (pink paint drips around the rims), the cans overflowing with pastel candy hearts. On another occasion the motif was gaily-colored kites and jelly beans; even the bar stools' cover fabrics change with each redecoration.

But it is Keepers' fantastic menu that captivates all diners. Plan to spend a healthy chunk of time just reading it.

Because the bill of fare—a good-sized "book" in a black ring binder—is so lengthy (and so entertaining) we'll let you discover it for yourself except for this excerpt describing one of Keepers' soups:

> Chilled Banana-Mandarin Bisque . . . get a load of this—light cream combined with pureed banana (oooh), to which is added creme de banana (oooh), light rum (oooh), ginger, brown sugar, whole mandarin oranges (oooh), and at the end a splash of gingerale to give it bite. Believe it or not, it's not all that rich. And if you plan to get drunk on it, three gallons will do it. We tried it.

Many of the items change from day to day but, as is obvious, Keepers' menu is always chatty, informative and amusing. Making a choice from all that's offered is pleasantly difficult: there are soups, appetizers, salads, hamburgers, quiches, omelets, desserts and an array of special drinks. On our most recent visit we started off with "The Celebration," a nicely tart concoction of champagne, orange and cranberry juices, which came with a stirrer of old-fashioned rock candy on a stick. As an appetizer we had "Livers and Other Strangers," chicken livers and water chestnuts wrapped in bacon served with very hot mustard, and "Chic Pea with Pepperoni Soup." The latter was perhaps the best we've ever tasted, deliciously spicy and chunky with pepperoni and potatoes.

Later we sampled Keepers' excellent chili, and the Boursin Quiche which came with a baked stuffed tomato, wedge of watermelon and a separate small salad of raw spinach, sliced mushrooms, real bacon bits and a delicate sweet-tart dressing. For dessert we indulged ourselves with pumpkin pie and an enormous slice of rich Chocolate-Chocolate Cake, layered with whipped cream and covered with thick, gooey chocolate frosting.

Prices at Keepers II are very reasonable; with one exception, the highest was a Crepe St. Jacques at $6.25. You can, however, run up a fairly sizeable tab if you order a number of items, all a la carte. The exception mentioned, by the way, is an appetizer—"Caviar and Champagne for Two: two ounces of Beluga caviar with garnish and Perrier Jouet Fleur de France (three days' notice, please) for $110"!

Keepers II is fun. The food is really excellent and innovative, service is deft; the ambiance is festive and friendly.

The place becomes very busy in the evenings, especially towards the weekend, and you may have to wait for a table. If you want to avoid a crowd, come in mid-afternoon on a weekday.

Keepers II is at 587 Bolton Street in Marlboro, (617) 481-5353. From Rte. 9 in Framingham, follow Edgell Road 4.6 miles to Rte. 20. Go left on 20 for 6.8 miles to Bolton Street (Rte. 85 north, but it doesn't say so). Bear right and go one mile; Keepers will be on the right. Hours are: Monday through Thursday from 11:30 a.m.-10 p.m., cocktails until 11:30 p.m.; Fridays and Saturdays from 11:30 a.m.-11 p.m., cocktails until 12:30 a.m.; closed Sundays. Only American Express or cash accepted, and no reservations are taken. Dress is casual, but dungarees are not permitted after 5 p.m.

Off the Beaten Path in Vermont

St. Johnsbury

Maple sugaring is one of New England's most traditional industries. In early spring, travelers throughout the region may spot evidences of the interesting enterprise—tapped trees with buckets attached or perhaps a plume of smoke in the distance indicating a sugar house in operation. Pure maple syrup, distilled from the sap of the sugar maple tree, is an expensive delicacy but well worth the price. It bears little resemblance to the less costly maple-flavored blends. And though the latter may be tolerated elsewhere, only the real thing will do for the true New Englander! Maple sugar candy, molded into a variety of shapes, is also a popular regional specialty.

Vermont, more than any other New England state, is associated with maple sugaring; in an average year it supplies about 65% of the nation's total maple syrup production. And **Maple Grove,** in St. Johnsbury, is the world's largest maple sugar factory. Visitors are invited to watch the sugaring process from start to finish, year-round. Guided tours of the factory, with free samples, are offered Monday through Friday except holidays from 8:30 a.m.-noon and 1:15-4 p.m. The Old Sugar House and Museum, with films and displays of old and new sugaring equipment, are open daily Memorial Day to late October from 8 a.m.-5 p.m. weekdays, 9 a.m.-5 p.m. weekends and holidays. The Maple Grove factory, Sugar House and Museum are on Rte. 2, at the east end of town.

In the early 1800s, a family named Fairbanks came to St. Johnsbury from Massachusetts. Thaddeus Fairbanks invented the platform scale in 1830; the company he founded, now world-wide, brought fame to St. Johnsbury and great wealth to the family. Public-spirited and generous to the core, the Fairbankses built (in addition to their own grand mansions) churches, schools and two remarkable museums, one for natural history and the other for art.

The Fairbanks Museum of Natural Science and Planetarium, constructed between 1889 and 1891, was created to house the extensive natural history collections of Franklin Fairbanks. An elegant red sandstone building fronted by two sculptured lions, the museum was designed by Lambert Packard in the Richardsonian style.

Inside, note the handsome arched oak ceiling, spiral stairways and oak and cherry woodwork; the building is worth seeing just for the magnificent craftsmanship that went into its construction. The collections are, however, equally as impressive—two levels of mounted birds and animals, minerals and fossils. If you have ever wished to see a moose up close, here's your chance: one of the awesome fellows is on view, along with a polar bear, a buffalo and countless smaller creatures including reptiles, insects and an absolute galaxy of birds.

Downstairs in the building's basement are hands-on displays of physical phenomena with buttons to push, lights to turn on and the like—great for children. A small museum shop is located on the first floor, just inside the entrance. The Planetarium, opened in 1968 in the tower, offers regularly scheduled shows. The museum, incidentally, maintains northern New England's largest weather data base; the weather station has been recording and transmitting data daily since 1894. Outdoors in summer there is a "live museum" with small animals, pond life, owls, hawks and reptiles all exhibited in natural settings. Monthly lecture programs and events are offered as well as workshops and classes in science, history and the arts, field trips, outreach programs and much more.

When Franklin Fairbanks built the museum, he chose an inscription for its massive fireplace that reads: "In wisdom hast Thou made them all." For that time, these words (taken from Cecil Frances Alexander's poem that begins "All things bright and beautiful"), showed a singularly modern understanding of the ecological relationship of "all creatures great and small." Today, almost one hundred years after its founding, The Fairbanks Museum—with its 19th-century character still perfectly preserved—is considered to be one of New England's finest centers of environmental education.

The Fairbanks Museum and Planetarium is at the corner of Main and Prospect Streets, St. Johnsbury, VT 05819 (802) 748-2372. In July and August, the museum is open Monday through Saturday from 9 a.m.-9:30 p.m., Sunday 1-6 p.m.; from September to June, Monday through Saturday 9 a.m.-4:30 p.m., Sunday 1-5 p.m. Admission is $2 for adults, $1.50 for senior citizens, $1 for children and $5 for families. Planetarium shows, admission $1, are presented in July and

August at 2:30 and 3 p.m. Monday through Saturday, 2:30 p.m. only on Sunday; from September to June, shows are given on weekends only at 2:30 p.m. Both museum and planetarium are closed on holidays.

The St. Johnsbury Athenaeum, another splendid gift to the town from the Fairbanks family, was founded in 1873. The oldest art gallery maintained in its original condition in the United States, the Athenaeum also serves as the town library. Horace Fairbanks purchased a substantial part of the gallery's art collection which includes a number of fine examples of the Hudson River school of painting. The Athenaeum, at 30 Main Street, St. Johnsbury, VT, is open Monday and Friday from 9:30 a.m.-8 p.m., Tuesday through Thursday and on Saturday from 9:30 a.m.-5 p.m.; closed holidays. There is no admission fee.

Montpelier/Waterbury/Stowe

Exploring craft shops is always an entertaining pursuit, especially when the weather dampens one's enthusiasm for outdoor activities. Vermont offers an abundance of native handicrafts and one of the most captivating collections may be found in a small cooperative shop in Montpelier. **The Artisans' Hand** displays the works of a large number of skilled craftspeople including potters, glassmakers, weavers and woodworkers. We were particularly enchanted with the Firerobin soft-sculpture animals and fish, one of which—a stuffed white corduroy rabbit with fabric-lined ears and a fluffy tail—left the shop with us.

Also irresistible were several handsome black and white alphabet posters by Mary Azarian, a talented Vermont printmaker. As appealing to adults as they are to children, each depicts a witty and imaginative scene of country life throughout the year. All 26 letters of the alphabet, by the way, are now available in book form: *Woodcuts by Mary Azarian,* published in 1981 by David R. Godine.

The Artisans' Hand is at 7 Langdon Street, Montpelier, VT, next to the river and not far from the State Capitol. Hours are 10 a.m.-5 p.m., Monday through Saturday.

Bear Pond Books, at the corner of Langdon and Main Streets, is another good place to visit in Montpelier. With an emphasis on poetry, philosophy, regional authors and titles, energy and natural living, Mike Katzenberg's Bear Pond is a pleasantly cluttered store with a rustic air. And around the corner, at 6 State Street, is **Magic Lantern Antiques.** Jo Moore, proprietor, calls her tiny shop "a treasure chest of antique and elderly items." Ideal for browsers, the shop's ever-changing wares are casually and invitingly arranged for easy poking about. There's no daunting "do not touch" feel to the place at all.

Should you develop hunger pangs while touring the area, we suggest a stop at the **Horn of the Moon Cafe,** a relaxed, unpretentious coffeehouse that thoughtfully provides reading materials for customers. Breakfasts include pancakes, a mushroom/onion/Monterey Jack cheese omelet served with the house's own whole wheat or raisin toast, and sauteed tofu with mushrooms, onion and tahini. For lunch or a light supper try one of the cafe's special soups, salads or sandwiches: perhaps chapati filled with broccoli and cheddar cheese, or a stuffed pita. Local and/or organic produce are used whenever possible, and no sugar. Despite the latter, the baked goods are delicious; we enjoyed an excellent apricot pastry accompanied by hot herb tea. Smoking, by the way, is banned at Horn of the Moon; the menu sternly warns that "Violators will be identified, located and shot on the spot!"

The Horn of the Moon Cafe is located at 8 Langdon Street, across from The Artisans' Hand, Montpelier, VT. Hours are Monday and Tuesday from 7 a.m.-3 p.m., Wednesday to Sunday 7 a.m.-8:30 p.m., Friday to 9 p.m., and brunch on Sunday from 9 a.m.-1 p.m.

If you cross the Langdon Street bridge over the river, you'll see a handsomely-renovated area called Jailhouse Common on the other side. The two-story brick structure to the right was once the old jailhouse, built around 1820. In addition to housing a large weavers' yarn and fabric shop, the building also holds a fine restaurant called **Tubbs Inn.** The entrance is around back.

An exceedingly attractive dining establishment, Tubbs Inn—owned and operated by Stephen and Judith Jones—opened in this location in September, 1980. Spacious, with high ornate tin ceilings painted in shades of blue, the restaurant is on two levels and seats about 80 people. (In summer, the outside deck is also used for serving.) The walls are warm-toned brick adorned with framed flower prints and other art; small pottery jars filled with daisies are on each table.

The day's menus are written on large blackboards with

eight specials plus sandwiches and salads for lunch, and nine or ten dinner choices. The latter might include broiled rack of lamb topped with garlic and herb butter or sauteed pork tenderloin with mushrooms, shallots, brandy, pate and cream. For dessert there may be Brandy Alexander pie, baklava, or Judith Jones' own invention—mocha and creme chocolate cheesecake. Tubbs' hot fudge sauce is renowned, too.

Tubbs Inn, at Jailhouse Common on Elm Street, Montpelier, VT, is open seven days a week (except for a two-week vacation, dates as yet undetermined). Lunch is served from 11:30 a.m.-3 p.m., snack-type foods are available late afternoon, and dinner is served until 8:30 p.m. weeknights, to 9:30 p.m. on weekends. Reservations are suggested: phone (802)229-9202. Prices range from moderate to expensive; Visa and MasterCard are accepted.

In Waterbury Center, a few miles northwest of Montpelier, there is one of the nicest cider mills we've ever encountered. Situated in a large, picturesque New England barn next to an old brick church, **The Cold Hollow Cider Mill** presses cider while you watch. Samples are offered, too—cold cider in the summer, hot spiced cider in chilly weather. The barn's rustic interior also holds a selection of gifts, Vermont crafts, books (some on cider-making or recipes using cider), and a host of delectable edibles. In the bakery section, for example, are such delights as whole grain breads, apple strudel and cobbler, and boiled cider pie—a rich pastry something like pecan pie made with cider, maple syrup and walnuts.

Be sure to pick up a jar or two of Cold Hollow Pure Cider Jelly; it's tart and absolutely delicious with cream cheese on toast or crackers. There are also jams of all kinds, marmalades, apple butter, maple products, Vermont cheese and—of course—apples and freshly-made cider. We like cider best when it reaches the slightly tingly stage, but there are those who prefer stronger stuff. If you'd care to try your hand at making hard cider at home, postcards sold in the shop offer the recipe. All that's needed are a barrel of cider, honey, an airlock, a cool temperature, and patience.

Cold Hollow Cider Mill, Rte. 100, Waterbury Center, VT, is open daily year-round from 8 a.m.-6 p.m.

To winter sports addicts, Stowe is synonymous with skiing. But the long-established resort town in the valley below Mt. Mansfield is an inviting place to visit at any time of the year—and is, by countless travelers. Most of Stowe's attractions, including scads of shops and restaurants and a goodly assortment of places to stay, are well known. Yet up in the hills beyond the town there is an establishment that we feel is reasonably off the beaten path. It is, moreover, startlingly unique.

Stowehof is not a typical New England country inn. Its style—Austrian with a strong touch of the whimsical—was created by the original owner/builder, interior designer and architect Larry Hess. The hostelry has expanded somewhat since our first visit years ago but most of its initial quirkiness is still happily intact. The drive leading to Stowehof provides nary an inkling of what you'll find on arrival; the road bends upward past lovely birch trees, tall firs and mountain meadows. The inn then appears in all its dramatic (to say the least) splendor: a soaring Alpine lodge complete with Old World bell tower and a section of sod roof, the entryway supported by the trunks of two giant maple trees.

Describing Stowehof is no simple matter—nothing is expected. The place is full of fascinating surprises. First of all, the inn meanders. It is multi-level with great open spaces mixed with cozy alcoves, nooks and corners: an inviting hodge-podge of places to read, play games or sit by the fire. Large picture windows offer marvelous views of Mt. Mansfield. Here and there you will note a tree, sometimes acting as a support, in other instances simply for decoration. There are books—lots of them, plus newspapers and periodicals—scattered about in niches and in the living room library. Upstairs, reached via a winding staircase or an elevator, is a game room designed to resemble the interior of an old Vermont covered bridge. The inn also houses a Tyrolean-style bar and a sauna.

Some 47 rooms and suites, each one different, all with private balcony or patio, are available for guests. A few suites offer fireplaces; some include a sitting area and dressing room. The rooms are done in an odd combination of rustic simplicity and overblown opulence, yet the views from windows and balconies more than make up for any lack of coherent taste.

Somehow, and we're darned if we can explain it, Stowehof's eccentric ambiance manages to effect a wonderful sense of comfort, relaxation, and fun.

The grounds are truly beautiful, winter or summer. Cross-country trails for skiing or snow shoeing begin right on the property and connect with some 50 miles of trails beyond. In summer guests may wander through the gardens, fish in a trout pond or roam through the adjacent woods over miles of walking trails. There are also a heated swimming pool, a putting range, and four all-weather tennis courts. Guests have member privileges at the Stowe Country Club with its 18-hole championship golf course.

Stowehof's cuisine is European-American; the dishes, prepared by a Swiss chef, are served in the handsome dining room with its beamed ceiling and fieldstone fireplace. Cocktails (including hot glühwein in winter) are served by the fire in the tap room. In summer, cocktails and lunch are offered out on the patio and beside the pool.

Stowehof is located on Edson Hill Road, Stowe, VT 05672 (802)253-8500. The inn is three miles from Stowe on Mansfield Road, then half a mile up Edson Hill Road. Stowehof is open year-round, and guests may choose a modified American Plan that includes lodging, breakfast, afternoon tea, early evening hors d'oeuvres, dinner and late evening coffee and pastry, or European Plan with room only. A 15% gratuity is added to your bill (no other tipping) and there is a 5% state tax. American Plan rates range from around $53-$75 per weekday per person, double occupancy; weekends and holidays are higher. Five-day midweek and two-day weekend specials are available.

Burlington/Bristol

Burlington, Vermont, is a city of steep hills, handsome old mansions, and spectacular views of Lake Champlain. It also has a large modern shopping mall that runs beneath the downtown area, and a fine collection of art in the Robert Hull Museum, part of the University of Vermont campus. In addition, Burlington offers a number of interesting places to dine. We will now take you on an eating tour of the city—from dawn to dusk, plus an after-dinner stop that ought not to be missed.

For breakfast or a mid-morning snack we recommend **Leunig's,** a coffeehouse at the corner of College and Church Streets. Classical music provides just the right background for cappucino, Irish coffee, brandied or spiced rum cider, or perhaps a noggin of hot milk and honey accompanied by a pastry.

For lunch, head for **The Rathskellar.** Walk along College Street; duck into the alley next to Bennington North Potters—you will find the restaurant in the back, downstairs. A cozy sort of place with stone foundation walls, brick pillars, barnboard and gigantic wooden beams, the Rathskellar is lit only by candles and lanterns. Rows of books may be seen on ledges and shelves. There is a good-sized main dining area, another smaller section in the rear up a few steps, and a few tables in the bar. For hungry diners, the buffet lunch is a great buy: included may be roast beef, hot chili, macaroni and cheese, five or so vegetables, all manner of salads, soup and fresh fruit—all for $3.50. Sandwiches include a deliciously gooey item called an English Delight (tuna, tomato, bacon and Swiss cheese) for $2.75; all sandwiches come with soup, french fries or potato salad. If corn chowder is offered, snap it up: it's excellent.

The Rathskellar, at 127½ College Street, Burlington, is open daily except Sunday for lunch, on Friday and Saturday night for dinner, and on Sunday for brunch. The regular menu is served from 11:30 a.m.-10 p.m., the buffet Monday through Friday from 11:30 a.m.-2:30 p.m., and Sunday brunch (with champagne) from 12 noon-3 p.m. American Express, Visa and MasterCard are accepted.

In case you abstained from having dessert at The Rathskellar (or even if you didn't), our next stop is **Ben & Jerry's Homemade** for an ice cream cone. Or a sundae. Situated at the corner of College and St. Paul Streets is what was once a gas station, Ben & Jerry's looks rather unprepossessing. But the ice cream, served by some 30 quality restaurants in the state, is very good indeed. It is made with all natural ingredients—100% pure Vermont milk and cream and lots of egg yolks, plus Irish sea moss and something called "guar" to keep the texture smooth. Flavors on any given day might include Oreo mint, gingersnap and grapenut, as well as the usual choices. Sundae toppings range from chopped Heath bars and M & M's to granola, jimmies, walnuts, honey, maple syrup or just plain hot fudge. Other goodies available are warm gingerbread with whipped cream, seven kinds of hot chocolate (such as mint, almond or mandarin orange), sodas and even egg creams. An unusual item is "fresh-squeezed hot lemonade with honey . . . 25¢ for anybody with an obvious cold."

Moving along towards dinner, come with us to **Pauline's**

Kitchen. Located in a smallish two-story brown and white house a few miles south of Burlington, Pauline's exterior is anything but auspicious. The place was, we discovered, originally a Greek diner with one kitchen in the front half of the present dining room, another in the rear, and a third upstairs in the owners' living quarters. Nowadays only one kitchen remains, turning out some of the finest food in New England. And the interior decor is charming.

Prints of old masters and French impressionists grace the brown and white plaid wallpaper; the lighting is soft—mainly from spotlights on the paintings and candles on the tables. Upstairs are three smaller dining rooms including one done in red and white with delicate stencilling on the walls. A lounge is planned for upstairs, too, but as yet is not under way.

Although Pauline Hershenson, the original owner, is still involved, the restaurant's present proprietors are Jayne Tozloski and her husband Chuck Collyer. In its fifth year of operation, Pauline's Kitchen continues to offer consistently superb food. As the menu changes weekly, we can't tell you exactly what to expect except that it will be delicious, and often creatively different.

On our last visit we started off with an appetizer called a "breakfast souffle," something like a Western quiche with bits of ham and a creamy sauce, and European beer soup with onions and melted cheese. An excellent tossed salad contained grated carrots, thinly sliced cucumber and crunchy croutons, with a zippy mustard dressing. Served along with these was a basket of hot popovers, bran/coconut bread and apple bread.

Entrees included several fish and beef dishes, shrimps scampi, chicken curry and an absolutely ambrosial mushroom, apple and cabbage strudel with a marvelous cider-tanged sauce that brought out the flavor of the apples. Our only (very minor) quibble would be to suggest another time that the strudel is perfect all by itself and doesn't need the accompanying rice and vegetable.

The price of the entree includes everything from appetizer to beverage and sherbet, but one may—for an extra $2—order a pastry or the house's special ice cream crepe with praline sauce. We chose the crepe, and also sampled a brownie topped with nut-chocolate-coated ice cream and fudge sauce. Prices are amazingly reasonable: the entire dinner for two, including a carafe of excellent California wine, came to $27. The restaurant also offers a "light dinner" of appetizer, soup, salad and those heavenly homemade breads for only $4.95—a nice idea and one we wish more restaurants would adopt.

Pauline's Kitchen, 1834 Shelburne Road (Rte. 7) is approximately four miles from downtown Burlington, on the left-hand side of the road. Hours are from 5:30-9 p.m. weeknights, to 9:30 p.m. on weekends; closed Monday. Reservations are advised: phone (802)862-1081. Visa and MasterCard are accepted.

You have now dined magnificently—all day long, if you've followed in our footsteps! We have one last suggestion to make: a postprandial drink at the **Harbor Hide-A-Way**. It is also on Rte. 7 south of Burlington, about one mile beyond Pauline's Kitchen on the other side of the road.

You will know the Harbor Hide-A-Way when you see it: look for a rambling building with a lighthouse top center and a Chinese pagoda roof to the lower left. This disparity of architectural styles is only a slight indication of what you'll find inside. The bar, and small lounge beyond, can only be described as astonishing. The table tops are decorated with an almost solid mass of glittery objects arranged on white aquarium pebbles embedded in lucite. Ours had pieces of antique jewelry, old watch bands and watches with no faces, and a bottle opener . . . plus a great deal more. Part of the ceiling and most of the walls are papered with a collage of magazine pictures; the ceiling nearest the bar is covered with business calling cards.

Gripping though these areas are, they are tame compared to the rest of the place. A labyrinth of dining rooms (the Harbor Hide-A-Way also serves dinners) contains—besides tables and chairs—the oddest, almost demented collection of items we've ever seen. For example: we noted costumes of armor, a number of elaborate chandeliers, artwork ranging from lush nudes in rococo frames to a "Pigs Are Beautiful" poster, an ornate upright coffin (with a slumped figure, a dummy, inside), dolls, a real skeleton, ships' figureheads, an ancient bird cage holding a stuffed parrot, stained glass, carved wooden screens, a stuffed mongoose complete with cobra (possibly real, we didn't want to know), a section of grotesque devils' and death masks, and —everywhere—guns. There is even a small cannon reposing upon a hearth, and in another room an enormous organ composed of various sorts of firearms (the keys are tiny pistols). Even before we spotted that organ we had the eerie feeling of having stumbled into the lair of the Phantom of the Opera. The rooms also include a small cave.

The owner of the incredible Harbor Hide-A-Way, a Burlington optometrist, is a well-known collector of guns. He also, it would seem, collects everything else in the world and eventually displays it all in his restaurant. We would estimate that there must be thousands of objects on view, each one more bizarre than the last!

Before we leave the Burlington area we'd like to mention an intriguing item about Lake Champlain. Whenever you have the lake in view, keep your eyes open—you might sight a sea serpent. A creature similar to Nessie, Scotland's Loch Ness Monster, supposedly lives in the watery depths. First reported by French explorer Samuel de Champlain in 1609, the beast (or something) has been spotted by more than 100 witnesses since then. Should you happen to spy a large serpentine object with a horned, horse-shaped head paddling along off shore, its name is "Champ."

South of Burlington just beyond Vergennes, a five-mile jog east on Rte. 17 off Rte. 7 will bring you to the small mountain town of Bristol. **Mary's,** on Main Street, is widely renowned for its food. A simple little place, the restaurant has a shining, well-scrubbed look, graced with pots of greenery. The reasonably-priced entrees may include scallopini of veal piccata at $7.75, or sauteed trout amandine at $8.45. Mary's desserts and wine list are exceptional. The restaurant is open Tuesday through Saturday for lunch from 11:30 a.m.-4 p.m. and dinner from 5-9:30 p.m. On Sunday a champagne brunch is offered from 10:30 a.m.-3 p.m. For reservations, phone (802)453-2432.

Across the street from Mary's there is a good bakery called **Wildflour Breads.** Usually about eight varieties of loaves are for sale including herb or Russian rye, plus old-fashioned doughnuts, bagels, turnovers and other baked goods.

Bristol is also the home of The Vegimals, unique "vegetables" and animals created by **Freemountain Toys Inc. at the Vegimill.** Our favorite is "Peas," a 17-inch-long deep green velour peapod; when unzipped five fat "pea brothers" may be found inside. Vegimals also include a 30-inch giant carrot, a blue velour can containing four "sardines," a banana inside its peel, a sectioned orange, a watermelon with three brown velour "seeds," and many more.

Freemountain Toys is located in an old building up the alley behind Mary's. We had hoped to find a retail shop on the premises—or at least to see the Vegimals being assembled. Most of the toys, however, are handcrafted by Vermonters in their own homes, then shipped out from the Bristol warehouse. We did spot a number of cartons containing such fetching components as unicorn horns, sheeps' ears, fish heads, etc., and a panda bear tapestry on the wall that read "Stuff It."

The women in the Freemountain Toys office told us that we weren't the first visitors to come to Bristol looking for a shop. A Swedish husband and wife, owners of several large toy stores, flew all the way from their native country to Boston, then trekked to Vermont and Bristol, just for that purpose. They had to content themselves with a handful of order forms. We acquired a full-color catalog. Just so you won't think we have led you to Bristol for naught, **Moynihan's**—a clothing store around the corner on Main Street—does sell Vegimals and other Freemountain toys and accessories (including their own special winged or horned hats) and sometimes even has sales on the items.

Countryman's Pleasure. Mendon, VT.

Mendon/Cuttingsville/Healdville

Mendon lies just east of Rutland, Vermont, on Rte. 4. Here we discovered a delightful restaurant called **Countryman's Pleasure**. Situated in a century-old Colonial house, the three-year-old restaurant is owned by Hans and Kathy Entinger, a charmingly friendly young couple. The decor, created by Kathy, is Early American and Austrian combining to create a cheerful "country" look. Two wood stoves offer extra warmth and a cozy ambiance in wintertime, and a taped mixture of Austrian, Swiss and classical music provides an appropriate background.

The cuisine, prepared by Hans, is mainly Austrian-German. Fourteen entrees include veal schnitzel Cordon Bleu and Wiener schnitzel, Bavarian sauerbraten, German bratwurst, stuffed chicken breast glazed with apricot, and seafood crepes Newburg. Prices are quite reasonable, ranging from $6.95 for the bratwurst to $13.95 for rack of lamb; all come with freshly baked rolls, a variety of garden greens, fresh vegetables and *spatzlis* (Austrian egg noodles). Two entrees offer a lower-priced, smaller serving for light eaters. There's a children's menu, too. The lengthy wine list includes German, Austrian and French selections. Champagne cocktails, Kir and spritzers are offered as aperitifs, and a wide variety of imported beers and ales is available.

Hans Entinger, a native Austrian, studied cooking and restaurant management in Switzerland and Germany. His breads, particularly the sticky buns with lemon or apricot topping, are superb. Kathy Entinger, in addition to teaching school (and when we visited, expecting a baby) maintains a large garden out back. Generally at least three of her fresh vegetables appear on the menu in season; there are also producing fruit trees and blackberry vines. Speaking of vegetables: Kathy told us that Hans, trained in the European manner of boiling vegetables to their death, soon learned to cook them lightly over here!

Countryman's Pleasure, on Rte. 4, Mendon, VT, is located three miles east of Rutland; you'll see the sign and the house on the right. The restaurant is open Tuesday through Saturday year-round from 5:30-9 p.m., closed Sunday and Monday. For reservations call (802)773-7141. The bar/lounge, called the Wayside Tavern, is open before and after dining hours. All major credit cards are accepted.

A bookshop in a "haunted" house, a stained glass studio, a

country inn and a 157-year-old cheese factory—all of these may be found in or near the tiny hamlet of Cuttingsville, Vermont. To get there, pick up Rte. 7B just south of Rutland and watch carefully for Rte. 103; it's only a short distance. Cuttingsville is about three miles further on 103.

We'll begin with the bookshop. Look for an enormous Victorian mansion on the righthand side of the road across from a cemetery. An artist, trying for the ultimate in Gothic thriller book covers, would be hard put to find any structure more suitable. Charles Addams would love it. But the gloomy old house, built in the 1880s, is—we're almost sorry to tell you—innocent of ghosts, goblins or other creatures that go bump in the night. At least that is what the tenants claim. Despite this disappointing news, the name of the establishment within is **The Haunted Mansion Bookshop.** Before we tell you about that, though, let us share with you the history of the house . . . and the impressive mausoleum in the cemetery across the way.

John P. Bowman, a wealthy tannery owner, lived the good life back in the mid-1800s. Then, sadly, his baby daughter died. Twenty-five years later he lost his only other child—another daughter—and his wife passed away soon after that. Stricken with grief, Bowman decided to build a fantastic memorial to his lost family. More than 100 sculptors, granite and marble cutters, masons and laborers worked for over a year creating the classic Greek mausoleum. The cost came to $75,000. The tomb's interior, finished in marble and mosaic tiles, contains marble pillars and Victorian chairs, brass candelabra, ornate urns and huge plate glass mirrors with marble frames—plus busts of the three adult members of the family and a statue of the baby. Outside is a replica of Mr. Bowman himself, a life-sized statue bowed with grief and carrying a cloak, silk hat, gloves, a huge funeral wreath, and a key. After the mausoleum was completed, Bowman landscaped the cemetery grounds, and then built the mansion directly opposite. Shortly thereafter—in 1885—he, too, died. It's really a pathetic tale, and we are surprised that the house *isn't* haunted, considering.

The Haunted Mansion Bookshop, which deals in old and used books, is owned by Clint and Lucille Fiske and their son Gary. As a boy, Clinton Fiske knew the Bowman Mansion well; he even mowed its lawns from time to time. After a

26-year-career working for an antiquarian bookseller in Rutland, he decided to open a shop of his own. The Bowman house, although it had fallen into disrepair, seemed the ideal spot—and, Fiske felt, deserved fixing up and preserving. The business began with only two rooms of books; now two floors of the house hold more than 50,000 volumes covering all subjects, with an emphasis on Vermontiana. In addition, there are collections of maps, prints and engravings, old bottles and a few antiques. And the mansion itself is fascinating to explore with its period-patterned wallpaper, unusual fluted and handpainted hall woodwork, massive rosewood staircase, stained glass, and heavy brass chandeliers.

The Haunted Mansion Bookshop, Rte. 103, Cuttingsville, VT 05738, is open six days a week from spring to late fall from 9 a.m.-5 p.m. The rest of the year visitors may call for an appointment: (802)492-3462.

The Castle Hill Stained Glass Studio is also on Rte. 103, back down the road from the Haunted Mansion Bookshop, across from the post office. The studio is located on the first floor of the old general store/post office building, complete with the original front porch and large windows. William and Mishcka O'Connor are the proprietors of Castle Hill, aided by artisan Jim Osborne. William O'Connor is a professional artist with more than 20 years' experience in stained glass. The studio designs and makes custom stained glass windows and lamps for homes, businesses, churches and synagogues, restores old windows and lamp shades and also teaches the craft.

Designs of windows already completed line Castle Hill's walls, and visitors may observe works in progress laid out on the studio's tables. Whoever happens to be there at the time will explain exactly what is going on. We learned a bit about some of the different kinds of glass used, such as "antique"—a handblown type made in Europe in the same manner as that once made for the windows of the ancient cathedrals. There are also "reamy glass," a German antique variety with a whipped effect, "English streaky glass"—an English antique with two or three different colors streaked through, and "opalescent glass" which is not blown, but rolled.

In case you don't feel the need for a stained glass window of your own, or can't afford one (they can be costly), the studio also has a selection of stained glass medallions for sale.

Castle Hill Stained Glass Studio, Rte. 103, Cuttingsville, VT 05738, (802)492-3525, is open to visitors year-round Monday through Saturday from 9:30 a.m.-5:30 p.m.

Just before the turn of the century, Cuttingsville was a thriving copper mining and granite quarrying community. Then there were nine inns and taverns where travelers could sleep and dine. Nowadays the town, not much more than a bend in the road, has only one inn—but it is a particularly appealing one.

The Shrewsbury Inn (Cuttingsville is a part of Shrewsbury) is deceptive. Outside it is an 1830-ish Vermont farmhouse; inside, the inn presents a decorating scheme that isn't at all what one might expect—a melange of styles and periods, comfortable furniture and colorful fabrics, and a host of intriguing collectibles. Lois Butler, owner and decorator, calls it "eclectic." We call it welcoming.

To the left of the front hall is a small dining room, the chairs covered in a stunning black and white material; on the tables are blue glassware and pretty arrangements of dried flowers. A pleasant living room opens up to the right of the hall; beyond is a cozy lounge where a human-size soft sculpture doll named Agnes Cornpepper reclines on red plaid windowseat cushions. (In summer, Agnes—neatly attired as always in her dress, hat and shawl—greets guests from a rocker on the front porch.) You'll note a number of English brass rubbings here and there, and a hall coatrack holding several medieval-style costumes.

A vivid red carpet runs up the stairs to the second floor where there are six guest rooms, four large and two small. Each is individually decorated with wallpapers in appealing stripes or patterns, lovely fabrics, and all manner of elegant small touches—including Mr. Finnegan, a handsome orange cat. He may be found napping in any one of the rooms, whichever suits his fancy at the moment. There are three full bathrooms with showers, all newly installed in one convenient cluster.

We weren't there at dinnertime, unfortunately, so can't report on the food except to tell you that the smells emanating from the kitchen were tempting. We did, however, ask if we could take along a menu. This request caused amused consternation, as the day's bill of fare is written out on a large blackboard. We settled for taking notes.

That day's offerings included asparagus parmesan, soups, quiche, Cornish game hen Dijonnaise, roast duckling diable and veal Marsala. The desserts included creme brulee and champagne au citron.

The Shrewsbury Inn is very much a family operation. Mrs. Butler's husband, a professor of engineering at Rutgers University, comes up on weekends and plans to start a wine cellar when he finds time. One son acts as chef, another does carpentry work around the house, and the daughter does a bit of everything, including baking bread and waitressing. A friendly, casual sort of place, the inn is an ideal getaway spot for anyone seeking the relaxation and simple pleasures of country life.

In winter, skiing and other snow sports are all available nearby. In summer there are hiking trails, and swimming at a beautiful mountain lake not far away. The scenic Mill River runs along just behind the house, and mountain slopes rise up beyond. Our lazy choice for a summertime diversion would be to wander up the road to the Haunted Mansion Bookshop, pick out six fat volumes, and then sit by the river and read. One note: there is no television set at the inn, so TV addicts will be out of luck.

The Shrewsbury Inn is on Rte. 103 just below the Haunted Mansion Bookshop, Cuttingsville, VT 05738; (802)492-3355. The rate per person is $18 per day including breakfast. No children under four, please. The inn is open year-round except for the month of November and from mid-April to mid-May. Dinner (at extra cost) is served Tuesday through Saturday from 6-9 p.m.; in summer lunches are also available.

If you continue along Rte. 103 southeast for about eight miles you will come to the **Crowley Cheese Shop** on the right. Besides the famed Crowley cheese, the store offers a nice selection of Vermont products such as pottery, woodenware, braided rugs, maple syrup and candy, homemade jams and jellies, and the like. To see Crowley cheese in the making, take the Healdville-Crowley Road beside the shop; it leads off Rte. 103 to the south.

A typically picturesque Vermont byway, the road—accompanied by a briskly running brook—winds past mountain farms and meadows, stone walls and lovely stands of birch and fir. **The Crowley Cheese Factory** will be on your left, about two miles along. Don't expect to find anything

Castle Hill Stained Glass Studio. Cuttingsville, VT.

resembling a modern factory, though. Watch for the sign and an old brown clapboard barnlike structure. In summer, flowers are in bloom all around the place. You will be greeted by Randolph B. Smith, a silvery-haired, handsome older gentleman with a winning smile. He is the proprietor of the Crowley Cheese Factory and your guide through the fascinating intricacies of cheese-making.

Alfred Winfield Crowley began making cheese way back around 1824, in the family kitchen. The present factory was built in 1882, and the Crowley family continued running the business until 1967 when Robert Crowley, Alfred's last surviving son, died. Randolph Smith then entered the picture, more or less by chance. After a career as an educator (including 25 years as director of the progressive Little Red Schoolhouse in New York City) Smith retired to Healdville, Vermont. Although he certainly wasn't looking for a new career, the demise of the last Crowley caused him to consider the fact that the cheese company, oldest in the state, would have to go out of business unless someone else took over the reins. So he did, with the able assistance of several long-time employees.

A century ago Vermont claimed to have more cows than people, and cheesemaking was one of its most prolific small industries. Almost every town had at least one cheese factory; many had three or four. Today only about half a dozen cheese-makers remain, all producing cheddar cheese. The Crowley Cheese Factory is the only one that makes Colby cheese, a form of cheddar. It is also the only one that makes the cheese by hand, using traditional 19th-century tools and techniques.

Basically the process goes like this: fresh milk is delivered early each day and poured into large vats, where it is heated and encouraged to sour. The custard-like curd that results is cut, raked and drained of whey. Next the curd is kneaded by hand, rinsed with spring water, packed into molds and pressed. Finally the wheels of cheese are sealed with hot wax and stored for aging.

Although the factory is open to the public all day, Mr. Smith suggests you try to visit between 11 a.m. and 1 p.m. It is during this busy period when the raking and kneading are done. We could go on for pages with details of the entire process, but that would spoil the fun of having Randolph Smith show you in person. We will, however, pass on a few interesting facts. The exceptionally delicious Colby cheese, as you will discover when offered a sample, has a different texture than true cheddar—softer, moister and more open. The aging period is two months for mild cheese, four months for medium sharp and six months to a year for sharp. "Just like people," Mr. Smith likes to say: "the older, the sharper."

Eight thousand pounds of milk are needed to make 800 pounds of cheese. Ninety per cent of the milk is lost in whey, which once was used to feed pigs but nowadays is mostly wasted. Whey, says Smith, is a fine natural food product, but not easy to process. The Crowley Cheese Company produces from 500 to 800 pounds of cheese each day, an awesome amount considering there are only four employees.

We feel that Mr. Smith deserves a great deal of praise for helping to preserve one of the few remaining examples of 19th-century industry. If he were Japanese, that country might well add him to its list of talented artists, musicians and craftspeople who are honored by being named "national treasures." Randolph Smith, however, is a New Englander and a Vermonter, typically modest and dryly humorous about his achievement. He took over the ownership of the cheese company, he notes, "on—appropriately—April Fools' Day!"

The Crowley Cheese Factory, on the Healdville-Crowley Road, Healdville, VT 05147, is open year-round from 8 a.m.-4 p.m. Monday through Saturday. The retail shop on Rte. 103 is open daily from 10 a.m.-5 p.m., 1-5 p.m. on Sunday, occasionally closed in winter. Wheels of Crowley cheese are for sale at both factory and shop. Prices range from about $12 for a 2½-pound wheel to about $21 for a 5-pound wheel, and cheeses may be ordered and shipped. The prices may seem steep, but Crowley Colby cheese is worth it—especially after you've watched the painstaking way in which it is made.

White River Junction/Quechee/Norwich

Unlike the other New England states, Vermont has no seacoast, and seafood restaurants are fairly rare. White River Junction, however, has a good one. **The Point Fishmarket Restaurant,** owned by Mr. and Mrs. Mike Guryel, is named for its location—on a point of land where the White and Connecticut Rivers meet.

The Point's decor is strongly nautical, with ships' lanterns and wheels, fish netting, ship models and a large figurehead. It's a comfortable, casual restaurant, with soft lighting and pleasant classical background music. In summer, meals are also served on an enclosed rear deck which offers a nice view of lawn and the river beyond.

The menu lists fifteen seafood entrees including haddock prepared in various ways, scrod, scallops, shrimp, filet of sole and Alaskan king crab. The fish, we were told, comes fresh from Boston. There are several beef items, too: steak, beef kabob, prime ribs (on Friday and Saturday nights only) and combinations of steak and seafood. The luncheon bill of fare offers sandwiches and burgers as well as steak and a smaller selection of seafood dishes. The Point's lobster stew is superb; a bowl, with salad and rolls, would make a perfect light meal. The tossed salad is also excellent, topped with a tangy herb dressing and grated cheese.

Mike Guryel and his wife are Turkish, which explains several items on the menu: *humus* served with Syrian bread as an appetizer, and a dessert list that includes baklava and Turkish Delight.

The Point Fishmarket Restaurant is located at 2 Maple Street at River Point Plaza, White River Junction, (802) 295-9222. It is open for lunch from 11:30 a.m. Monday through Friday and for dinner Monday through Saturday until 10 p.m.; closed Sunday. Prices are moderate; Visa and MasterCard are accepted.

In Quechee, just west of White River Junction, there is a marvelous Scottish import shop. **Scotland By the Yard** sits high on a hill above the road, reached via a steep, curving driveway. In summer visitors may observe a small herd of authentic Highland cattle and a flock of black-faced sheep grazing placidly on the grassy hillsides back of the shop.

The attractively rustic store professes to offer the largest range of registered Scottish tartan fabrics in North America, and we don't doubt it for a minute! The tartans are magnificent to see in all their colorful array. **Scotland By the Yard** also offers a wide range of luscious sweaters, authentic kilts, outerwear, lambswool scarves, hats galore (including handsome handknit Aran tams), ties in a choice of more than 600 tartans, pottery, blankets, walking sticks, traditional *skean dhus*, and clan crest jewelry. There are books about Scotland's clans and tartans, tins of shortbread, whiskey-flavored candy, oatcakes and other delicacies and even a selection of Scottish soaps and colognes. In the background Scottish music softly plays; records are also for sale. The shop, on Rte. 4, is open daily year-round from 9 a.m.-5 p.m. It is three miles west of scenic Quechee Gorge.

Shopping International may be a familiar name to readers who have received the firm's mail order catalog, offering imports from all over the world. The company's headquarters are in Norwich, Vermont, a few miles north of White River Junction, and a large selection of its wares are on display in a handsomely designed retail shop on the premises.

More than 30 countries are represented, with some 3000 items on view in a colorful international "bazaar." An Asian Pavilion holds exotic treasures from India, Africa, the Middle East and Southeast Asia; a bamboo-roofed Oriental Bazaar contains Japanese pottery, Hong Kong porcelain, brass from Taiwan and rosewood, soapstone carvings and lacquerware from Mainland China.

Linen and woodenware from Finland, Norwegian pewter, Swedish crystal and Danish teak are all displayed in the pine-paneled Scandinavian Mart. The rustic European Shop offers items from Greece, France, England, Russia and Spain; the Mexican Plaza, done in wrought iron and stucco, has hand-wrought tin, glassware, pottery, bark paintings, wall hangings and basketry from Mexico along with handicrafts from Peru, Guatemala, Uruguay and Bolivia.

The Fashion Boutique includes gaily-patterned apparel from Greece and India, shawls and serapes from around the world, fine handbags, and a large collection of jewelry. In addition, there's a small section offering seconds.

Shopping International, Inc., is located on Rte. 5, Norwich, about five miles north of White River Junction. The shop is open year-round Monday through Saturday from 9:30 a.m.-5 p.m.; from June through December it is also open on Sunday from 1-5 p.m. Visa, MasterCard and American Express cards are accepted.

Off the Beaten Path in New Hampshire

The Lake Winnepesaukee Area

Lake Winnepesaukee has two distinct personalities. Its western shore is a summertime hive of activity, thronged with visitors drawn by a multitude of attractions. Amusements of all sorts are available at Weirs Beach, and there are countless shops, restaurants, and places to stay. We, however, prefer the quieter eastern side of the lake. Even in midsummer its winding country roads are less traveled; there are farms, woods and old cemeteries, and only a scattering of small villages.

Wolfeboro/Melvin Village/Center Ossipee

The charming old resort town of Wolfeboro is situated at the southeasternmost point of Lake Winnepesaukee; smaller Lake Wentworth lies directly to the east. The **Mount Washington,** offering 3-hour cruises of the lake, picks up passengers at Wolfeboro as well as other stops along the shore. The **Wolfeboro Railroad** departs from a depot right off the main street for a wonderfully nostalgic ride through the countryside in old coaches drawn by a steam locomotive.

Wolfeboro is also the home of the **Hampshire Pewter Company.** The foundry is in a modest gray wooden building on the lefthand side of the road on Rte. 28 heading northeast from town. The firm, small as it is, produces some of the finest pewter in the world—handmade by skilled craftspeople using centuries-old techniques. Visitors are invited to watch the fascinating process in all its stages from mixing alloys to final polishing.

Most pewter pieces manufactured nowadays are *spun:* sheets of prepared pewter are shaped around wooden molds and then finished. At Hampshire Pewter the pieces are *cast* and *turned:* molten metal is poured into bronze molds and then the pieces are turned and finished by hand. The base metal used, mixed on the foundry's premises, is a blend of five "virgin" metals: tin, copper, antimony, bismuth and silver. No lead is added. The mixture results in an exceptionally fine pewter called "Queen's Metal," originally developed in the 16th century for use by English royalty. Today only two other companies make Queen's Metal—one in

London, the other in Malaysia. Objects made of the metal are stronger and more resilient than those made with other types of pewter; they even ring when tapped. And they possess that lovely soft sheen we usually associate only with antique pewter.

Hampshire Pewter was established in 1973 by two master pewterers from England. When they returned to their native country a few years later, Joe Santoro, previously a marketing director for Corning Glass, purchased the firm. It is, Santoro is proud to state, the only American company that trains master pewterers; the guild apprentice system takes seven long years to complete. Prestigious jewelry shops throughout the United States carry Hampshire Pewter's wares, and many noted people such as former President Gerald R. Ford and the late Shah of Iran have commissioned pieces. In addition to creating its own collection, the company makes reproductions for a number of museums—including New York's Metropolitan Museum of Art.

Wait, if you can, until after you've watched the pewterers at work before you explore the small retail shop upstairs. When one understands the entire process, the beauty of the finished pieces can be much better appreciated. The selection includes goblets, plates and bowls, vases, candlesticks, napkin rings, spoons and much more, all attractively displayed throughout the shop. We were particularly drawn to a magnificent pewter lamp, unfortunately too costly for our budget. The prices are steep, but undeniably worth every penny: any of Hampshire Pewter's collection will become a treasured heirloom.

The Hampshire Pewter Company, Rte. 28, Wolfeboro, NH 03894, (603)569-4944, is three miles from downtown. Free tours are given on the hour from 9 a.m.-3 p.m., Monday through Friday, year-round. The shop is open Monday through Saturday from 9 a.m.-5 p.m. MasterCard and Visa are accepted.

Now follow Rte. 109 north from Wolfeboro along the lake for ten miles to tiny Melvin Village. The village is part of Tuftonboro, and the Tuftonboro Historical Society—an interesting place to visit—is located in an old schoolhouse on the righthand side of the road. Mrs. Marion Horner Robie, local historian extraordinaire and curator of the museum, satisfied our curiosity concerning the name "Melvin."

Old records report that a 1725 expedition against the Indians, led by one Captain John Lovewell, included two brothers named Melvin. The expedition is believed to have camped along the north shore of Winnepesaukee. Local tradition says that early settlers in the region found a tree with "Melvin" carved on its trunk, very likely by one of the brothers. The name Melvin was first officially used in 1771, applied to the village's stream that runs down the mountainside, under Rte. 109 and out into the lake.

In any case, Melvin Village is there today, to all appearances merely a quiet little hamlet consisting of a general store, a post office and church, a small restaurant and gas station, and the Willing Workers Hall. For most of the year the village maintains its peaceful mien, but for one weekend each November, it becomes the scene of an exciting event called **Salmon Stripping.** Let us explain.

The salmon spawning season in Lake Winnepesaukee begins about the third week of October and continues to the end of November. The lake's salmon are the landlocked variety which do not swim upstream to spawn. So the New Hampshire Fish and Game Department puts out pound nets to trap the fish; then the salmon are transferred to pocket nets near the mouth of the Melvin River. Around 700 salmon, out of a total population of about 40,000, are collected. On the second or third weekend in November, the public is invited to watch as the actual stripping of the salmon takes place. (You'll have to check with the New Hampshire Fish & Game Department, 34 Bridge Street, Concord 03301, (603) 271-2501, for the actual dates, as they differ each year.)

Some 80 female and 40 male salmon are selected and placed in holding tanks upstream. During public days the Fish and Game people strip the eggs from the females into pans where they are mixed with male milt, which fertilizes the eggs. Then the fish are released: landlocked salmon do not die after spawning as other species do. The eggs are stored in glass bottles and taken immediately to hatcheries where they spend a year and a half growing into young salmon; finally they are used to restock New Hampshire's lakes.

Brook Dupee, section leader, Cold Water Research and Management Division of the Fish & Game Department, is enthusiastic about the annual salmon stripping operation. "The nicest thing about the procedure," he says, "is that the fish aren't caught to be killed and eaten, but to help add to the state's salmon population instead." The process, incidentally, has been going on (in other areas as well) for about 120 years. In Melvin Village the operation takes on a decidedly festive air. Some 500 to 600 people come to cluster around the holding tanks and watch, and to enjoy hot coffee, sandwiches, chili, and delicious homemade baked goods offered for sale at the Willing Workers Hall across the road. The money earned all goes to local charities or for a variety of worthy community causes.

Melvin Village has also been immortalized in verse, by the poet John Greenleaf Whittier. The ode called "The Grave By the Lake," published in 1867, rambles on for 26 interminable stanzas of which we'll now quote the first two for your edification (They are best appreciated when read aloud):

> Where the Great Lake's sunny smiles
> Dimple round its hundred isles,
> And the mountain's granite ledge
> Cleaves the water like a wedge,
> Ringed about with smooth, gray stones,
> Rest the giant's mighty bones.
>
> Close beside, in shade and gleam,
> Laughs and ripples Melvin stream;
> Melvin water, mountain-born,
> All fair flowers its banks adorn;
> All the woodland's voices meet,
> Mingling with its murmurs sweet.

By now you have the general drift. The giant referred to in the first stanza was an Indian; his **burial spot** (marked by a plaque) is located on a rise above the lake next to the old cemetery beside the village church. The gracious Mrs. Robie provided us with the following information: in the early 1800s when the road leading to the lake was being built, a wall of granite blocks was constructed to hold back the dug-up earth. (The area is now the cemetery.)

During the digging operation, the skeleton of a gigantic Indian —in a sitting position—was found buried in a sandy bank. The large skull was removed and brought to the general store for exhibition. Later it was returned to the grave, but since has probably disintegrated after having been subjected to air and daylight. As for the unknown Indian's being buried sitting up, at least one New Hampshire Indian mound unearthed by archaeologists has provided evidence that the bodies of tribal members were customarily placed in a sitting position around a common center, facing outward.

Just down the road below the village (towards Wolfeboro on Rte. 109), there is an especially inviting gift shop called the **Hansel and Gretel.** It's a lot larger than it looks from the outside; in addition to the central display areas, a number of mini-shops open off from the room to the left, each devoted to a particular type of item such as books (mainly on New England), candy, children's toys and clothing, and cards and wrappings. One is a year-round Christmas shop. The Hansel and Gretel Shop offers a well-rounded selection of gifts, handmade crafts, miniature dollhouse furniture, and jewelry. A fishpond in the middle of the shop is an irresistible lure for children. They are provided with rods and allowed to cast for plastic fish; a small prize (at no charge to parents) is awarded to each youthful fisherman.

Winnepesaukee is the largest lake in New Hampshire, but its 72 square miles—dotted with almost 300 islands—are not easily viewed all in one piece. The shoreline extends for some 183 miles, curving around innumerable wooded coves and inlets. As you drive you will glimpse parts of the lake, but elevation is required for a truly panoramic view. One of the best vantage points is from the **Abenaki Tower,** just off Rte. 109 south of Melvin Village across from the entrance to the Wawbeek Colony. From its summit you will see the northeast end of the lake, Melvin Bay, and—to the right—eight-mile-long Moultonborough Bay. The 45-foot-high tower is a ten-minute walk beyond the parking lot, up a marked, wooded trail.

For a spectacular view of the entire lake, drive over to the **Castle in the Clouds** in nearby Moultonborough. The castle, formerly the country estate of a wealthy industrialist, stands on a promontory overlooking Lake Winnepesaukee; the White Mountains are clearly visible in the distance. To reach it, follow Rte. 109 north from Melvin Village for seven miles to the junction with Rte. 171. Turn right on 171; the entrance gate for the castle is three miles further, followed by a scenic two-mile drive to the top. The castle and grounds are open weekends only in May and June from 9 a.m.-5 p.m., daily in summer from 9 a.m.-6 p.m. and during fall foliage season from 9 a.m.-5 p.m.; closed the rest of the year. The admission charge includes a tour of the castle.

Off The Beaten Path in . . .

An excellent place to dine or stay overnight while you're in the area is the **Hitching Post Inn and Restaurant,** in Center Ossipee. Although it may be reached via numbered routes (the long way around) we'll take you there by the most direct method—over the mountain. (Much more fun, especially in the dark!) From Melvin Village follow Rte. 109 south; at the junction with Rte. 109A, veer left. Look sharp for a red brick schoolhouse; then take a left onto Ledge Hill Road, proceed through Tuftonboro Four Corners (where **Dow's Antique Shop** is, we hear, highly recommended) and down the other side of the mountain to Center Ossipee. Bear right on Old Rte. 16; the Hitching Post Inn is at the corner. Innkeepers Roberta and Herb Lawson are a cordial couple guaranteed to make your visit a memorable one.

Once a stagecoach stop, the inn is about 150 years old. We'd love to tell you more about its history, but strangely enough, little is known. This is not to say it doesn't *have* a history—it does. The trouble is, Mrs. Lawson explained, a certain degree of jealousy exists between several of the towns hereabouts as to exactly which one owns the old records, and in effect, this rivalry prevents researchers from getting at the facts.

We can, at least, tell you that the Hitching Post is delightful and the food is very good indeed, served in one of several pleasant dining rooms all with fireplaces or wood stoves. The menu features seafood, sirloin steak and prime ribs of beef. The Chef's Casserole with shrimp, scallops, lobster and haddock, or Baked Lobster Pie (both prepared with lots of butter and wine) are outstanding. On Friday, Saturday and Sunday evenings there is also a lavish Smorgasbord Buffet laid out in the Sleigh Room; for only $6.95 ($4.95 for children) guests may serve themselves as often as they wish from a vast array of items including homemade soup, beef, pork, fish and fowl, salad and fresh fruit (from the separate salad bar) and a variety of desserts. Regular entree prices range from about $5.95 to $10.95; anyone desiring only a light repast may choose the salad bar alone along with soup and hot rolls, for $4.50. The dessert list includes strawberry shortcake, homemade pies, cheesecake, sundaes, and grapenut or Indian pudding.

Upstairs the Hitching Post Inn has six comfortable guest rooms, sharing two baths. The rooms, furnished in Colonial fashion, are $20 double occupancy, additional persons $4 extra.

The Hitching Post Inn and Restaurant, Old Rte. 16, Center Ossipee, NH 03814, (603)539-4482, is open year-round. The restaurant, with full bar service, is open daily for luncheon (offering sandwiches and specials as well as complete meals) and from 4 p.m. for dinner.

Gilford/Laconia/Meredith

To reach the western side of Lake Winnepesaukee from Wolfeboro, follow Rte. 28 south to the junction with Rte. 11 and take 11 north. Rte. 11B just beyond Glendale will take you directly to Weirs Beach, but we'll make a short side trip, staying on Rte. 11 into Laconia. Just outside of Laconia, in the Gilford area, you will see an Alpine-like structure off the road to the left. Look for the sign: **Pepi Herrmann Crystal.**

Please don't dismiss it, thinking it merely another tourist trap selling those ubiquitous blown glass souvenirs. On the contrary, the shop offers a glittering display of exquisite handcarved crystal, some of the finest examples made today. The rustic Austrian-style setting creates a splendid backdrop for the prismatic array, set on tables, shelves and in small alcoves. There are bowls and plates, vases, decanters and stemware—carved in traditional patterns like "Snowflake" or "Stars," or contemporary designs such as "Bamboo" and basketweave "Caro." Also on view are candleholders, paperweights, cruets, pendants and tiny crystal creatures such as swans, mice and even crystal porcupines.

Visitors to the shop are invited to descend the steps to the basement, where Josef "Pepi" Herrmann creates his works of art. Herrmann, a large, bearded Austrian, is a master crystal cutter, one of the very few practicing today. He studied at the Glasfach Schule in Kramsach, Tyrol, for four years, then spent seven more years perfecting his art at Riedel Glas, a Tyrolean glass manufacturer. Here in New Hampshire, Herrmann first worked as a ski instructor at nearby Gunstock before opening his own crystal shop.

No glass blowing is done here; the un-cut pieces are imported from Europe. Herrmann uses only the finest crystal, with a lead content of about 30% which gives it extra weight, an exceptional luster, and a bell-like ring. He and his fellow artisans follow the old, traditional techniques of crystal cutting: designing, roughing, smoothing and polishing all by hand. Each piece is first marked with a design, and deep cuts are made using a stone grinding wheel.

The primary coarse cuts are then finely cut with wheels of smaller gradation. The deeper the cuts the more brilliantly the piece reflects light.

Inevitably, the cutting process involves some breakage and we—nosy as always—wondered what happens to the ruined pieces. They are thrown out, and the same goes for any imperfect specimens—for Pepi Herrmann tolerates nothing but the best. He signs and dates all of his work, and it's expensive. A 9-inch snowflake-patterned bowl costs $249, a peacock plate $448, a champagne flute $45. A few modestly-priced items are also for sale, however a tiny paperweight for $15, a crystal key ring for $6. Porcupines will run you either $44 or $65, depending on size.

Pepi Herrmann Crystal is on Gilford East Drive just off Rte. 11, about 1½ miles east of Laconia, NH; (603)528-1020. The shop is open Monday through Saturday from 10 a.m.-5 p.m., year-round.

A short distance north of Laconia there is an elegant-looking restaurant called **The Hathaway House.** We describe it this way because we weren't able to see the inside, at least not very much of it. It was closed the day we were there, so we had to content ourselves with peering through the windows. The handsome late 19th-century house, situated on the shore of Lake Winnisquam, is light chocolate-colored clapboard with white trim. Our glimpses of the interior showed several small dining rooms charmingly decorated with patterned wallpaper and draperies, deep gold tablecloths and brown napkins. Bouquets of silk flowers graced each table and we spotted a crystal chandelier in the hallway, and several marble fireplaces. An attached barn also has a dining area. Because the place seemed so attractive, we asked several local residents about it. They told us that the food is good, and the prices not terribly steep. Therefore, even though we missed trying it out in person, we feel The Hathaway House is worth mentioning.

The Hathaway House Restaurant is about one mile north of downtown Laconia on Rte. 11/3; the actual address is 1106 Union Avenue, Lakeport, NH; (603)524-8840. Luncheon hours are 11:30 a.m.-2:30 or 3 p.m., dinner from 6-9:30 p.m. Monday through Saturday, Sunday brunch from 10 a.m.-1 p.m. Off season (winter) the restaurant is closed on Sundays and Mondays.

New England, surprisingly, boasts ten working vineyards—and one of them is in New Hampshire. **The White Mountain Vineyards and Winery** are located 2½ miles south of Laconia on Rte. 107 (at the corner of 107 and Durrell Mt. Road.) Between May 1 and August 31, visitors are welcome to stop in for wine tasting and tours of the winery and vineyard. In Meredith, north on Rte. 3 from Laconia, there is another of the company's vineyards—on the righthand side of the road one mile south of town. New England's oldest commercial vineyard, it was planted in 1964 as an experiment to show the suitability of the region for viticulture.

White Mountain Vineyards produces 15,000 cases of wine each year. Mostly hybrids, the wines also include fruit wines, Catawba and sherry. A recent judging awarded White Mountain Vineyards silver medals for its Foch 1975, Seyval Blanc and Pink Catawba, bronze medals for Lakes Region White, Aurora Natur and Cream Sherry, and an honorable mention for Lakes Region Rose.

Directly beside the vineyard on Rte. 3 in Meredith is a shop called **Stem to Stem.** White Mountain Vineyards' products plus other native American wines, and imported wines as well, are for sale here. The store also offers a large selection of wine glasses and accessories, and gifts. Stem to Stem is open daily from 9:30 a.m.-5 p.m., except from January through April when it closes on Mondays and Tuesdays.

Ashland

The hilly little town of Ashland lies northwest of Meredith; it is a roundabout ten-mile drive on Rte. 3 north. In Ashland, we recommend an uncommon restaurant called **The Common Man.** Look for a red brick house with a fanlight over the door right on Main Street (Rte. 3). It will be on the righthand side; parking is available in a lot across the street.

The Common Man is extremely popular and you can expect to find people waiting in line in the entrance hallway. A tray of cheese and crackers helps while away the time. There is also a tiny shop called **Out of Hand** that offers antiques, gifts and New Hampshire crafts, including an appealing assortment of stuffed animals. The restaurant's decor is country provincial with low beamed ceilings, a brick chimney and several wood-burning stoves; on the walls are framed prints and a collection of antique plates. In addition to the main dining area there are several smaller rooms; one in the front of the building is decorated with wooden rolling pins and old signs. A wooden-treaded circular staircase leads upstairs to a comfortable lounge where another wood stove offers warmth in wintertime.

Sandwiches at The Common Man are full-fledged meals; we particularly enjoyed the hot sliced turkey on homemade honey-wheat bread, topped with a delectable white wine sauce. Some of the other choices are roast beef on sourdough bread with Marsala gravy, and the "Monte Cristy" —piled with turkey and ham, tomato, cucumber, Swiss and blue cheese. An item called "Cheese Dream" looked tempting, too: ham, turkey, mushroom or broccoli baked in a cheese sauce, topped with sliced tomatoes, bacon and Swiss cheese. The soups are homemade and hearty; on our last visit the day's special was an elegant cream of broccoli and potato.

Regular entrees range from seafood and beef to veal Cordon Bleu, chicken Florentine and vegetable-k-bob. Your waitress will bring a wooden recipe box to the table for inspection. Inside are descriptions of the various dishes, the ingredients handwritten on ring-bound cards. In general, we'd say that the cuisine is simple country cooking, nicely done with herbs, spices and a great many unusual touches. The restaurant's wine list isn't lengthy, but does offer a well-rounded selection.

Desserts are rich and completely irresistible. Mud Pie is a specialty—coffee ice cream in a graham cracker and fudge crust smothered with hot chocolate sauce and whipped cream. Other choices include old-fashioned strawberry shortcake with homemade biscuits, brownie sundae, ice cream-filled puff, spicy, warm Indian pudding, and cheesecake with fresh strawberries.

The enterprising owner of The Common Man also operates **Mame's** in Meredith and **The Pine Shore** near Holderness, and has recently opened a new place in Ashland called **The Curtis House.** The last, we were told, serves very special gourmet dinners, and reservations are a must.

The Common Man, Main Street (Rte. 3), Ashland, NH, (603)968-7030, is open for lunch Monday through Saturday from 11:30 a.m.-2 p.m. and dinner daily from 5 p.m.-9 p.m., year-round. Luncheon prices are very reasonable, ranging from sandwiches at $1.50 or $2.50 to specials and entrees from $2.75 to $5.95. Dinner prices are higher, but still quite moderate. American Express is accepted.

Southwestern New Hampshire

This lovely section of New Hampshire is usually called the Monadnock Region, named for its highest mountain. The geological term "monadnock," meaning a mountain that stands alone, comes from this isolated peak. If you've never climbed a mountain, Monadnock is the one on which to begin. Only 3165 feet high, it is reasonably easy to master —supposedly it is the most-climbed mountain in the world.

The area also includes **The Cathedral of the Pines.** It is in Rindge, two miles east of Jaffrey on Rte. 124, then two miles south on a marked road. An open-air "cathedral," it is simply a pine-covered knoll with rows of wooden benches, and a stunning view of Mt. Monadnock beyond the austere stone altar. Underfoot a thick layer of pine needles muffles all sound except the murmur of the trees and occasionally the sonorous tones of an organ.

The Cathedral of the Pines is dedicated to the memory of Sanderson Sloane, a young man who was killed in World War II. Sloane's father created the memorial, with the help of people from all over the world who sent stones to help build the altar. Later a scattering of other stone buildings were added, and a memorial bell tower. Even though the Cathedral of the Pines is visited by thousands of tourists each year, it still remains a remarkably beautiful and peaceful sanctuary—a place of worship for people of all faiths. There is no admission charge, but contributions are welcomed. The Cathedral is open to the public daily from 9 a.m.-4 p.m. in May, June, September and October, and from 9 a.m.-5 p.m. in July and August; closed the rest of the year.

From Jaffrey, take Rte. 137 north to Rte. 101 and go left to Dublin (two miles). A back-country road from Dublin leads to **Harrisville,** an early 19th-century mill village virtually untouched by time. Camera buffs will love it. There are a picturesque millpond complete with ducks, one or two other ponds, and a cluster of handsome red brick buildings. Water from the millpond still runs downhill under a series of old textile mills. Several of the structures once again house a variety of businesses; the most appealing (and currently the one of most interest to visitors) is **Harrisville Designs,** a shop for weavers. Inside you'll find hand looms in all sizes, beautifully shaped from durable New Hampshire pine. Several of the looms show work in progress. Loom kits to construct at home, and loom accessories, may be purchased. Yarns and fleece in a rainbow of shades are also available.

One of New England's nicest old inns is located not far from Harrisville, in Hancock. Follow the road east to Rte. 137; Hancock is seven miles north on 137, at the junction with Rte. 123. **The John Hancock Inn**, operated by Glynn and Pat Wells, dates back to 1789. The inn's wide front porch offers a row of old-fashioned rocking chairs, great places to sit and watch the leaves on the trees, or the odd bird. You won't see much *other* activity! Hancock, named for John Hancock, who once owned property here, is a very small town—consisting of a main street, a group of old white houses and a village green. It's a delightfully restful spot in which to break a trip or spend a relaxing few days.

The inn's interior includes a comfortable living room with a fireplace, an intimate lounge, and several attractive dining rooms. The food is first-rate, attracting hosts of diners especially on the weekends; reservations are advised. Upstairs there are ten pleasant rooms for guests, decorated in period style.

The John Hancock Inn is on Main Street, Hancock, NH 03449; (603)525-3318. Breakfast is served from 8-9:30 a.m., lunch Monday through Saturday from noon to 2 p.m., dinner from 6-9 p.m. and Sunday from noon-2 p.m. and 5-8 p.m. The inn and restaurant are open year-round. MasterCard and Visa are accepted.

Skiers please note: the **Crotched Mountain Ski Area** in nearby Francestown is often overlooked. The majority of skiers tend to head further north to the better-known mountain resorts, yet Crotched Mountain offers fine skiing, is usually less crowded, and is only a day trip from Boston. Consisting of two areas—Crotched Mountain East and Crotched Mountain West—the facilities include eleven beginner, eight intermediate and seven expert trails, a double chair and a Poma lift, rentals, downhill instruction, and a base lodge and lounge. To reach Crotched Mountain Ski Area from Hancock, take Rte. 127 north to Rte. 202 north, then Rte. 47 east for five miles. (Crotched Mountain is 15 miles northeast of Peterborough.)

Grandmother's House in Francestown, at the foot of Crotched Mountain on Rte. 47, is a charming place to dine.

Open year-round, it is situated right at the fork in the road, in a nice old brown clapboard house with white trim. The ambiance is warm and rustic with wood-paneled walls and beamed ceiling. By day the dining room is bright and cheerful, the sun shining through small-paned windows onto white linen tablecloths and fresh flowers on each table.

John H. Trappe, who took over the restaurant from Anna Yoss, the original "Grandmother" of Grandmother's House, maintains its long-established tradition of good food. The bill of fare still includes a number of German specialties such as sauerbraten with potato dumpling, wiener schnitzel, and pig's knuckle with sauerkraut, as well as seafood, beef, duck and Cornish hen. The luncheon menu offers several entrees plus hot roast beef sandwiches, chicken livers and bacon on toast, and omelets. Prices range from $7.50 to $11.50 (lower for lunch); entrees come with potato and vegetable. During the busy seasons—ski, summer or foliage, and on weekends—reservations are essential: phone (603)588-2355. Dinner seatings are at 6 and 8:30 p.m. Cash or personal checks with identification only are accepted; no credit cards.

From Francestown, pick up Rte. 136 east to New Boston (seven miles) and then Rte. 13 heading northeast towards Goffstown. **The Davis Scenic Highway** runs along Rte. 13 for three and a third miles. Despite its grandiose designation as a "highway," it is actually just a very pretty stretch of country road edged by rambling stone walls and ranks of silvery birches; the stony Piscataquog River runs alongside. There is a wooded picnic area, too, on the bank of the stream.

The Davis Scenic Highway, like the Cathedral of the Pines, is a memorial to a young man who died in battle. Ronald Charles Davis of New Boston, a sergeant in Company B of the 8th Infantry Regiment, was killed in Vietnam in 1970. Three years later a special session of the New Hampshire legislature named the highway in his honor. We think that this scenic bit of road makes one of the finest—and most poignant—memorials anyone could wish.

Off the Beaten Path in Maine

Cape Neddick

The state of Maine, among its multitude of scenic and other attractions, also contains an astonishingly large number of good restaurants. Seafood, of course, is the predominant offering—especially along the coast—and the Maine lobster is served in countless dining establishments ranging from elegant to the ubiquitous lobster shack. We suggest you try the latter; they're far from fancy, but the lobsters are freshly captured from the sea and, as a rule, are somewhat less expensive. But the icy Maine waters also provide marvelous clams, and some of the best fried clams we've ever tasted are served at El's on Rte. 1 in Cape Neddick.

El's has been in business for 36 years. For 35 of those years it was merely a tiny clam shack by the side of the road, a takeout place only, operated by Jack and El Ritchie. Then Mr. Ritchie died, and Mrs. Ritchie—El—considered either selling the business or closing it down permanently. Fortunately for fried clam lovers (who have been beating a path to El's in vast numbers for almost four decades) she did neither. Because the old shack needed a great many repairs, Mrs. Ritchie decided to build a new El's, right next door. The original structure, although no longer in use, remains as a local landmark.

The current El's is much larger, with a bench for take-out customers and booths for those who wish to eat inside. It is a bright, spotlessly clean place run in a remarkably efficient manner by El, her daughter, and her son-in-law. Fried clams, the house specialty, are sold in mountainous quantities —served piping hot and covered with a light, crisp batter. Delicious onion rings are almost as popular as the clams, and patrons may also choose fried shrimp, haddock, scallops, or chicken nuggets.

Lobster or clam rolls are available in season, and for the rare soul who doesn't care for seafood, there are hamburgers and hot dogs, accompanied by El's excellent french fries. Beverages include soft drinks, coffee and iced tea; there are no desserts, not even ice cream. The prices, considering the cost of seafood nowadays, are quite reasonable.

El's is located on the west side of Rte. 1 in Cape Neddick,

just north of York Beach and south of Ogunquit. From the Maine Turnpike heading north, take Exit 1 to York; heading south, take Exit 2 to Wells. In summer El's is open daily from 11 a.m.-11 p.m.; closed on Wednesday. In winter, hours are Friday from 4-8 p.m. and Saturday and Sunday from noon-8 p.m.; closed the rest of the week.

Portland

Portland is a pleasant old city, much of it built on high land overlooking Casco Bay. Down near the waterfront you'll find **The Old Port Exchange**, an area of hilly streets lined with beautifully restored brick-front Federal and Victorian buildings. It's great for walking and browsing, and there are benches where one may sit and observe the passing scene. In summer, flowers bloom in profusion. Shops of all kinds offer crafts, clothing, gifts and nautical brass items, and there is a large selection of fine restaurants.

Our favorite is **The Vinyard**, a small bistro on Middle Street. In earlier incarnations the building housed a luncheonette and a motorcycle repair shop. The Vinyard, which opened in 1979, is owned by Jaap Helber, a charming young Dutchman. There are only eight tables; two are situated in cozy niches next to the windows facing the street. The walls are painted a soft blue-gray shade that complements the Corsican blue tablecloths. Fresh flowers grace each table and—an unusual touch—each piece of dinnerware is different.

As its name implies, The Vinyard offers a superb wine list; sixty per cent of the wines are imported. Helber does not serve cocktails, but diners may order an aperitif of sherry or Cinzano, or cordials for after the meal. The food is marvelous. The menu changes nightly, always including appetizers and a soup or two, three entrees, salad, and two desserts. On our last visit we enjoyed a delicately flavored cream of cauliflower soup followed by sauteed breast of chicken and filet of sole with oyster sauce. The entrees also included tournedos of beef with artichoke hearts and Bearnaise sauce. A side dish of broccoli and cubed potatoes accompanied the main course along with an excellent house salad.

Desserts were a spicy cardamom cake with freshly whipped cream, and a sinfully rich, dark, Viennese chocolate torte—we chose one of each, and shared. On other nights there might be Lemon Leontine, a lemon cake with mocha filling, blueberry streusel or homemade baklava. Entrees range from $8.50 to $12; soups and desserts are extra.

As small as The Vinyard is, there is no feeling of being crowded or rushed. Service is deft and unobtrusive, the background music is classical, and the atmosphere is one of low-keyed elegance and romantic intimacy. The last is irresistible. One evening, Jaap Helber told us, a couple came in and ordered dinner but seemed far from happy about it. They shared no conversation, and the husband—a dour, burly sort of man—appeared ill at ease. Slowly, however, the food, wine and gracious surroundings began to take effect. By the end of the meal, to Helber's amusement, the gentleman's mood had mellowed to a startling degree, and the couple left not only talking to one another but holding hands!

The Vinyard is located at 111 Middle Street, Portland. Look for a tiny wooden-fronted building with red trim and a scalloped canopy. Hours are from 6-9:30 p.m.; closed Monday. In future years, Jaap Helber may also close the restaurant for the month of February. Reservations are advised, particularly during the summer season: phone (207)773-5424. Visa and MasterCard are accepted.

We're always delighted to discover a really good place for breakfast, and **Di Philippo's Ye Olde Pancake Shoppe** is one of the best around. It is on Congress Street, Portland's main downtown thoroughfare. Larger than it appears from the outside, the restaurant offers both table and counter service. The decor is simple but comfortable with plaid carpeting and Tiffany-style lamps. Waitresses and owner are all friendly folk, very cheering on a rainy morning. Twelve kinds of pancakes are served including silver dollar, blueberry (with berries in the batter and blueberry compote on the side), pineapple, bacon bits, apple, etc. At least a dozen varieties of omelets are also on the menu, plus eggs prepared any way you want, and sandwiches. Prices are very reasonable: eggs, sausage, home fries and coffee, for example, are only $1.90.

Di Philippo's Ye Olde Pancake Shoppe, at 617 Congress Street, Portland, ME (207)773-2785, is open weekdays from 5 a.m.-2 p.m., weekends from 6 a.m.-2 p.m.

Chinese restaurants are still rare in Maine, but Portland's 150 or so dining establishments do include one that we found well worth recommending. Called **Hu Shang**, it offers

Off The Beaten Path in . . .

Hunan, Shanghai, Szechuan and Mandarin cooking. Hu Shang's original quarters, at 608 Congress Street, are—to be perfectly honest—less than inspiring. In the very near future, however, the restaurant will be moving to another location on Brown Street, near the Civic Center. The new Hu Shang, we hear, will be much larger and fancier, with an expanded menu. We trust that the food will continue to be as good as in the past, and that the prices will remain as moderate as before.

A word of caution about the spicy "hot" dishes offered. They may be ordered (a) mildly hot, (b) medium, (c) very hot, and (d) or (e) incredibly hot. And they mean it. We suggest medium, unless you enjoy pain or have an asbestos throat.

As there is no large Chinese community in Portland, we were curious about the nationality of Hu Shang's cooks. The food is obviously authentic but, for all we knew, it could have been prepared by anyone trained in Chinese cuisine. Our waitress admitted that of the six chefs in the kitchen three are Chinese, two are Vietnamese, and one is a Cuban refugee. As one might imagine, there is a slight language problem, but it has been solved to everyone's satisfaction.

Hu Shang (Restaurant). Portland, ME.

The Chinese cooks communicate with the Vietnamese through one of the former who speaks Chinese, Vietnamese and English. The Cuban, who speaks none of the above, is given directions by numbers!

You will have to check the phone book for the new Hu Shang's address on Brown Street. The restaurant's hours will probably be the same, though: Monday through Thursday from 11:30 a.m.-9 p.m., Friday and Saturday to 10 p.m., and Sunday from 4:30-9 p.m.

There are, of course, other things to do in Maine besides eat, and one of the most pleasurable is to head out to sea in a small boat. Several sightseeing tours of Casco Bay and its islands are available year-round out of Portland, but we think the most interesting—and different—is a trip on the **U.S. Mail Boat**. The only passenger service of its kind in the United States, the mail boat cruise offers an intriguing glimpse of daily life on the Maine islands. The boat is the islands' lifeline, the islanders' only source of supplies and (unless one owns a private vessel) the only means of transportation to or from the mainland.

Our seagoing venture took place on a sunny morning in early spring—if March can accurately be called spring in Maine. The air is always nippy on the water, even in summer, and the further out we went, the chillier it got. But we braved the cold and stayed on deck (clenching chattering teeth) throughout the journey. There is a heated cabin for less intrepid voyagers. Along with the ticket for the cruise we received a handsome map of Casco Bay devised by the famed historian Edward Rowe Snow. The map traces the boat's route and provides a wealth of historic information about the islands and Bay, sundry shipwrecks and ocean battles, and many other colorful items.

In addition, a friendly young crew member named John Pearson gave us a running commentary whenever he had time between chores. Casco Bay is liberally dotted with islands, called the Calendar Islands because there are, supposedly, 365 of them. There aren't, but the count depends on how one defines an island. The most common definition, according to Pearson, is a piece of land that still remains visible at high tide—and the Bay, in addition to a number of inhabited islands, has many that are only barren chunks of rock. Our cruise took us to half a dozen of the larger islands including Little Diamond and Great Diamond, Peak's, Long,

Cliff and Chebeague. And we passed close to the Bay's most awesome sight, Fort Gorges, a massive fortress begun in 1858 that was designed to protect Portland's inner harbor. Pearson also pointed out the areas where wildlife may sometimes be observed: harbor seals, dolphins, ospreys, and even rare bald eagles.

Watching the offloading of supplies is fascinating. We saw a refrigerator and heavy piles of construction material delivered, all without the slightest hitch. But our voyage took place on calm seas; on rough days the unloading can be hair-raisingly tricky—crates of eggs or tomatoes, for example, having to be hurled ashore into waiting arms. Breakage, surprisingly, is almost nil.

The mail boat cruise ordinarily takes about three hours round trip, depending on the number of passengers and their destinations, goods to be delivered and—of course—the mail. It is a breezy, salty and thoroughly enjoyable experience . . . except, we will admit, possibly in the depths of winter in a raging Nor'Easter!

The U.S. Mail Boat Cruise leaves from the Casco Bay Lines terminal, Custom House Wharf, Commercial and Pearl Streets, Portland, (207)774-7871. Boats depart at 10 a.m. and 2 p.m., year-round. The fare is $6.55 for adults, $4.65 for children.

For a panoramic view of Portland Harbor, Fort Gorges and the islands in Casco Bay, follow Congress Street east to the **Eastern Promenade**. If you're up early enough you might see a magnificent sunrise. An even grander vista is available from the top of the **Portland Observatory** on Congress a few blocks to the west of the Promenade. Constructed in 1807 on Munjoy Hill as a signal tower to relay messages between incoming ships and the city, the observatory is open throughout the summer months. For sunset watchers, the **Western Promenade** (on the other side of Portland's peninsula) looks towards open countryside and the White Mountains. And six miles to the south of the city, 41-acre **Two Lights State Park** off Rte. 77 in Cape Elizabeth, offers spectacular views of open ocean and pounding surf.

Sabbathday Lake/Poland Spring/South Paris/Bryant Pond

From Portland, Rte. 26 angles towards the northwest. From late fall through early spring the road is blissfully tranquil and untraveled, meandering through gently rolling countryside. In the summer, however, it is the major highway for Canadians heading towards Maine's beaches, and the traffic is often heavy. Despite this seasonal fuss and fury, Rte. 26 is our choice—for it leads to **Sabbathday Lake**, one of the two remaining Shaker communities in America.

In the 19th century, the Shakers, founded by Mother Ann Lee of Manchester, England, were a flourishing religious group with 18 large communities scattered through New England, upper New York State, Ohio and Kentucky. The name "Shaker" came from the group's style of worship, in which the Brothers and Sisters literally shook their whole bodies as they danced. They called it "shaking out evil." They believed in simplicity, perfect peace and goodness, and in celibacy.

Obviously, a celibate group can continue in existence only so long, and eventually membership began to decline. The spartan life of the Shakers appealed to fewer and fewer people, and today only a handful of elderly Sisters remains —here at Sabbathday Lake and in Canterbury, New Hampshire.

In 1957, when there were only about 50 Shakers left, a decision was made, reluctantly, to close the group to new members forever. Although dedicated followers may still come and even spend their entire lives within the community, they cannot legally become Shakers. We assume that this was a protective measure to prevent any unscrupulous souls from taking over Shaker lands and wealth. (When the last Sister dies, the money will go to charity and for upkeep of the group's museums and other buildings.)

Several unofficial Shaker brethren do reside at Sabbathday Lake, including Brother Ted Johnson, who is director of the museum. He has lived and worked there since the 1960s, giving all he earns to the community. Some five Sisters are still in residence, and the community carries on its traditional ways in most respects: farming, growing culinary herbs and teas, and making the Shakers' famous rosewater. Nowadays the residents usually wear modern dress, and their unique dancing is a thing of the past. But there is still a lot to see at Sabbathday Lake. The old meeting house is an architectural gem, and the museum is fascinating. Also on the property are several barns and outbuildings, and a handsome brick central dwelling house with great chimneys and a cupola. There are orchards and gardens, too.

Everything the Shakers did was done well, and Shaker furniture was some of the finest ever produced. Models of functionalism and grace, each exquisitely crafted object was designed for a specific need or use. A number of museums around the country maintain collections of Shaker furniture, and the pieces are often copied by contemporary craftsmen. As Sabbathday Lake, visitors may see examples of the furniture, and in the gift shop may purchase Shaker-made products such as herbs, spices and teas, handmade candy and gifts, books about the Shakers, notepaper with samples of their "spirit drawings," and records of Shaker songs sung by the Sisters.

One of the songs, we think, charmingly exemplifies the Shakers' beliefs:

> 'Tis the gift to be simple,
> 'Tis the gift to be free,
> 'Tis the gift to come down where we ought to
> be,
> 'And when we find ourselves in the place just
> right,
> 'Twill be in the valley of love and delight.'

Sabbathday Lake is an experience not to be missed: it is a community of joyous serenity, of faithful attention to simplicity. Yet the Shakers' zest for life and work, and their love for one another, are not such simple gifts after all. There's also an air of poignancy, especially evident in the Shaker cemeteries. In one, a central stone marker states, simply, "Shakers . . . 1842-1885."

Sabbathday Lake Shaker Community is on Rte. 26, Sabbathday Lake, a few miles north of Gray and just before Poland Spring. The gift shop, museum and reception center are open to the public from Memorial Day to Labor Day, Tuesday through Friday from 10 a.m.-4 p.m.

Continuing along Rte. 26 you'll come to Poland Spring, where the famed Poland Spring sparkling water (now owned by Perrier) is bottled. The old Poland Spring resort still welcomes guests; the original hotel, which burned, has been replaced by a new structure. Up behind is an amazing edifice, **The Maine State Building**. Set high on a hill, it offers a grand view of the surrounding countryside, but it is the odd architecture of the place that really catches the eye. Created to represent the State of Maine at the 1892 Chicago

World's Fair, the building was later dismantled and returned here for use as the resort's library and art gallery. (It is currently undergoing restoration, and wasn't open when we were there.)

But even the exterior is worth seeing: the first floor is octagonal, made of Maine granite and marble with neo-Byzantine arches. The second floor, of white wood, is square with four turrets and a number of porches; the third floor, under the roof, is circular. The building, which looks like something out of a Maxfield Parrish painting, is generally open from May to November.

Maine contains a number of towns with unlikely names such as Poland, Norway, Sweden, Denmark and Mexico. It also has a Paris—plus a South and a West Paris. None of the Parises, sad to say, bears any similarity to the proud city in France, but South Paris (located just beyond Norway on Rte. 26) *does* boast an authentic French restaurant.

Maurice's has been providing superb French cuisine for a number of years, and has developed an outstanding reputation. Situated on the main street of South Paris, it is a simple white clapboard house set against a spruce-covered hill. Inside are an attractive dining room done in the French colors of blue, white and red, and a small adjacent bar with wicker stools and two tables.

The menu offers a nice choice of appetizers including superb house pate, escargots Bourguignonne, quiche and smoked salmon. Eight fish and eight meat and poultry entrees are offered—such as Coquille Saint-Jacques, Escalop de Veau Flambes or Poulet Sautee au Chablis. There are also weekly specials, such as fresh salmon in season. The dessert list includes freshly-made pastries as well as Mousse au Chocolat and fresh fruit.

Maurice's, 113 Main Street (Rte. 26), South Paris, is open year-round Tuesday through Saturday from 5-10 p.m., for Sunday brunch from 10 a.m.-2 p.m. For reservations, phone (207)743-2532. It is fairly expensive, ranging from $6.95 to $26 (the latter for Chateaubriand for two). Sunday brunch items, all a la carte, are mostly under $3. All major credit cards are accepted.

Over in Bryant Pond, 17 miles northwest of South Paris, there is a very different sort of dining establishment called **The Boiler Room**. We like it very much. First of all, it's on the shore of a beautiful little mountain lake. Come if you can in daylight so as to enjoy the view from the dining room windows. Next, the building itself is a delight. Originally the powerhouse for a clothespin factory, the old brick structure has been ingeniously restored to display much of the massive machinery that once ran it. Owners Joe and Louise Robiller spent three years on the renovations before they opened the Boiler Room Restaurant and Lounge in late 1979.

Outside, even the restaurant's sign is composed of cogs and gears welded together. Scattered around the grounds are more bits of machinery, forming unique outdoor stabiles, and the entrance is flanked by massive old boiler doors and saw blades. Inside there is a vast, open central lobby with a lounge to the right; the dining room is up a few steps to the left. More boiler doors separate the lounge from the lobby, and inside the lounge is an enormous 1890 steam engine. It works, too—or could. An impressively large piece of machinery, the engine once powered all the other equipment in the plant via a belt and pulley system. The Robillers spent six weeks sandblasting and painting the engine, and it is now very handsome indeed. The tables in the lounge were originally spools for the pulley system, wooden ones about five feet across and ten inches thick.

Perhaps the choicest part of the restaurant, though, is the Wine Cellar. Reached via a curving brick stairway, it is a long, narrow area with a beamed ceiling. Cozy booths are set into arched brick alcoves. Attached to the wall in each alcove is a portion of a wooden wine barrel, with a spigot. (The wine comes from a source up above via a hose, but who cares—it's the effect that counts.) Guests tap their own wine, a Paul Masson Chablis, and keep tabs on how many glasses they drink. Everyone's on the honor system. Another clever touch: the folded napkins are clipped with wooden clothespins. We didn't ask, but we would like to think that they were some of those made in the old factory up above.

Joe Robiller was born and raised in Germany and the Boiler Room's cuisine reflects his ancestry, offering a number of German specialties. Sauerbraten, rouladen, konigsberger klopse, schnitzel, knackwurst and bratwurst are some of the offerings, plus a delicious pickled herring salad made with apples, beets, pickles and potatoes. But even the American-style items have German names: the hamburger, for instance, is "Gehacktes Rind." Louise Robiller creates all the desserts, including German chocolate cake, blueberry-topped cake, and admirable filled cookies. (If you want to try her cooky plate, get your order in early, as they disappear rapidly.)

The Boiler Room Restaurant and Lounge is on Rte. 26, Bryant Pond, ME. For reservations phone Bryant Pond 100. That's not an error. Bryant Pond has the only crank phone service still in operation in the United States! The Boiler Room is open seven days a week year-round from noon-10 p.m. on weekdays, to 11 p.m. on weekends. Prices are moderate. Visa and MasterCard are accepted.

If you head west from Bryant Pond, you'll come to the start of The White Mountain National Forest, and the state of New Hampshire. We, however, are going in the other direction—via back roads. Rte. 219 (off Rte. 26 a few miles east of Bryant Pond) will get you started. From there on, it's your choice as to which routes to follow to reach Maine's coast once again, ending up in the Camden area.

Camden

Camden, one of the prettiest towns anywhere in the United States, is particularly notable for its harbor into which tumbles a picturesque waterfall. It also boasts a number of interesting shops and good restaurants. Among the latter, we highly recommend **Yorkie's.**

The original "Yorkie," before he retired and opened the restaurant, was a clown with the Barnum and Bailey Circus. Today Yorkie's is owned by Sam and Barbara Marques. Located in a small red clapboard house on a hill above the harbor, it is a sunny little place with tables, booths and a tiny five-seat counter. An open deck out back is planned for the future, to be eventually glassed in for year-round serving.

Sam Marques is Portuguese; he relates that he grew up abroad and as a child had no television or similar amusements to occupy his time. So he read a lot, and took up baking as a hobby. Later in life he decided to try baking as a full-time occupation and for several years operated a near-by pastry shop. Sam now creates Yorkie's pastries and there is a take-out bakery counter filled with his wares just inside the restaurant's front door. On any given day the selections might include luscious French cream horns, fresh strawberry pie, Danish pastries, excellent breads, and cookies.

Yorkie's menu offers an inventively different assortment of items for either breakfast or lunch; the restaurant is not open for dinner. Pancakes include blueberry, pecan, chocolate chip and potato. Steak and eggs, blintzes, and a variety of omelets such as ham and cheese, broccoli cream, and crabmeat are also offered. For an unusually good version of French toast, ask to have it made with Sam Marques' Portuguese sweet bread.

Frittatas are a house specialty, concocted with three eggs and a melange of other ingredients. The "Farmer," for example, is made with roast beef, potatoes and onion, the "Portuguese" with linguica, potatoes and onion—both topped with a pool of melted cheddar cheese. They're delicious and very filling, sort of a cross between an omelet and scrambled eggs.

Sandwiches, in addition to the usual hot dogs and hamburgers, include a host of interesting combinations like linguica and cream cheese on an English muffin, peanut butter and bacon, broccoli in herbed mayonnaise topped with sprouts, and cream cheese with ham and pineapple on Portuguese sweet bread. The only problem with Yorkie's, in fact, is the difficulty one has in choosing!

Yorkie's is located at 44 Chestnut Street in downtown Camden, ME (207)236-3156. It is right off Rte. 1; look for the sign. The restaurant is open weekdays from 5:30 a.m.-2:30 p.m., on Saturday from 8 a.m.-2 p.m.; closed Sunday. The bakery is open Tuesday through Saturday from 8 a.m.-5 p.m., Sunday from 8 a.m.-noon; closed Monday. Currently, Yorkie's is open all year but in the future it will be closed in either March or April for vacation.

For dinner, **The Helm** is one of the best restaurants in the Camden area. From its name, travelers might assume it to be just another seafood establishment; it even has a take-out section attached to one side where fried clams and similar items are sold. But the French-owned Helm, as well as offering American dishes, serves authentic French cuisine—and it is always excellent. On a recent visit the day's specials included a hearty French beef stew and an interesting casserole of ham, mushrooms and endive, topped with melted cheese. The restaurant's coffee is exceptionally good, too. Our waitress said that many people comment on its quality; she confided that a brand made by Victor is used.

In addition to the main dining area, The Helm has a small greenhouse addition where meals are served in the summertime. It is built out over a tumbling stream that runs along behind the building, and at night the water is floodlighted. The restaurant is very popular locally and closes fairly early in the evening. So we suggest that you either make reservations or plan to dine as early as possible.

The Helm is located on Rte. 1, one and one-half miles south of Camden, on the righthand side of the road if you're heading south. Hours are from 11 a.m.-8:30 or 9 p.m.; closed on Monday. The restaurant is also closed during the winter months, from November to early April. For reservations, call (207)236-4337. Prices are moderate; no credit cards are accepted.

Rockport/Rockland/Damariscotta

Rockport, one mile south of Camden, is the home of **Andre,** New England's most famous harbor seal. For a number of years Andre spent his winters at Boston's New England Aquarium and then—each spring—swam all the way back to Rockport. Nowadays the seal lives in Maine's chill waters year-round. In summertime he generally surfaces in Rockport's harbor early each evening to put on a well-attended show for visitors.

Not far from the town landing, a fraction of a mile up the hill beyond Rockport's center, is **Anne Kilham Designs.** Watch for the sign; the house is at 142 Russell Avenue on the righthand side of the road. Anne Kilham or her daughter Annie will usually be on hand in the studio during normal business hours. In addition to block prints and drawings, Anne Kilham Designs include a selection of handsome note cards, postcards, gift enclosures and several delightful Advent calendars.

Kilham's themes are mostly typical Maine scenes: a lighthouse in black and white; a red country farmhouse surrounded by deep snow; a steepled village church overlooking a harbor; a lobster shack with wooden lobster pots, upended dory and a lone seagull. Others are native flower motifs such as black-eyed susans or blooming lupine, or blueberries set against a background of birchbark. Some of the note cards have holiday themes: a fish shack with Christmas wreaths for sale or an old opera house under glittering stars, its lighted windows decorated with wreaths. Our favorite Advent calendar portrays a snowy scene with a rambling New England stone wall and falling snowflakes, each flake hiding a little animal.

Off The Beaten Path in . . .

In Rockland just down the coast, pay a visit to **The Farnsworth Museum**. Its full name is the William A. Farnsworth Library and Art Museum, and it houses a distinguished collection of regional paintings, drawings, prints and sculpture. Miss Lucy Copeland Farnsworth established the museum, in memory of her father, through a trust fund under her will. In one of the galleries, there is a wonderful portrait of Miss Lucy and her brother as small children. The Farnsworth opened in 1948 and the collection continues to grow, spanning more than two hundred years of American history. Included are late 18th-century native folk paintings, examples of the great 19th-century American artists such as Winslow Homer, Gilbert Stuart, Thomas Eakins and George Inness, and 20th-centruy works by Edward Hopper, Rockwell Kent, John Marin and William Zorach, among others. There is also an extensive collection of paintings by N.C., Andrew, and Jamie Wyeth.

The building itself is noteworthy, with a circular staircase that extends upwards for three floors, warm oak wainscoting and oak parquet floors. Two galleries on the main floor offer changing exhibits, and another—with ship models and other nautical items—is devoted to Maine's maritime history. The library, which takes up the entire south wing, is particularly

The Farnsworth Museum. Rockland, ME.

inviting. The high-ceilinged, paneled room was created around a magnificent marble fireplace; its mantel, originally in the U.S. Supreme Court Building in Washington, D.C., was designed by Charles Bulfinch. The library contains a number of fine antiques, a stunning crystal chandelier, comfortable chairs and couches, and a comprehensive art reference collection including a section of books illustrated by Maine artists.

There is also a Museum shop with gifts, crafts, reproductions of many of the Farnsworth's works, and original paintings and prints. Right next door to the museum is **The Farnsworth Homestead**, considered to be one of the finest Victorian homes in the country. It is listed in the National Register of Historic Places and is open to the public.

The Farnsworth Museum and Homestead are located at 19 Elm Street in the center of Rockland, just off Rte. 1. If you're traveling south, take Union Street to Elm; you'll see the sign for the museum. If traveling north, take Museum Street to the left, another left on Union, and go left again on Elm. From June 1 to September 30, hours are from 10 a.m.-5 p.m. Monday through Saturday, 1-5 p.m. on Sunday. From October 1 to May 31, the museum is closed on Monday; it is also closed on legal holidays. The Farnsworth Homestead is open June 1 to mid-September from 10 a.m.-5 p.m. Monday through Saturday, 1-5 p.m. on Sunday. Admission to both museum and homestead is free.

From Rockland, follow Rte. 1 south. As you're passing through the Waldoboro area look for **Moody's Diner** on the left. It's an institution in the region and a good place to stop for coffee and a snack. Next, watch for the sign to Damariscotta.

This pleasant little town has a number of fine shops for browsing, and one of the best delicatessens we've ever encountered. **Cohen's Deli and Bakery** is on the main street in Damariscotta and offers a raft of deli items plus a tempting array of imported delicacies, and all manner of teas. The soups, all homemade, are marvelous; the sandwiches and other specialties are equally as good. But, it it's available, the piece de resistance is "Lucy's Chocolate Cake." The portions are gigantic, easily enough for two, and the cake is scrumptious—dark moist chocolate with a creamy dark chocolate frosting.

On Winter Street in Damariscotta (up the hill to the

right—ask anyone if you don't see it) there is an unusually charming gift shop called the **Victorian Stable**. It is open only during the summer months. Once a real stable, an elegant one, the rustic barnlike building houses a choice selection of gifts and Maine crafts. Some are displayed in small rooms, originally the stalls, leading from the main open area. Up the stairs in the rear is another room devoted to the unique "dolls" of local artist Effie Lewis. Every one is a work of art, a character study of a real person, and they're enchanting.

Inside the Victorian house attached to the stable is the **Willoughby Restaurant and Coffee House.** Richard Watherwax, the proprietor, told us that the house was constructed in 1847 by Elbridge Norris, a builder of clipper ships. The ornate tin ceilings, we were fascinated to learn, were originally intended to repel rats! Nowadays, even if there were any rodents around, Mr. Watherwax's cats would make fast work of them. The restaurant, which was established in 1979, has two attractive dining areas, and we noted three handsome fireplaces: one marble, one granite, and one of onyx. The Willoughby serves lunches, dinners and Sunday brunch, and on Saturday night there is live classical music.

The luncheon menu offers three sandwiches including melted cheese and ham with green pepper, chicken salad, and bacon, lettuce and tomato, plus lasagne and a quiche and crepe of the day. There are also soups and a variety of salads. Dinner entrees include sauteed scallops, filet of fish baked in white wine, beef curry and beef burgundy, and chicken Provencale or chicken with artichoke hearts. Desserts range from chocolate mousse and pastries to carrot cake, blueberry cheesecake parfait, and yogurt with honey

RICHARD WATHERWAX'S

Willoughby

Water Street   (207) 563-5992   Damariscotta, Maine and nuts. The lengthy beverage list offers freshly ground coffees of various sorts, including Cappuccino and Mochaccino, teas, cider and hot chocolate, and after-dinner drinks, cocktails, wine and beer.

The Willoughby, on Water Street, Damariscotta, is open from 11:30 a.m.-10 p.m. daily in summer, varying hours in winter. Reservations are necessary in season: call (207) 563-5992. Prices are moderate. No credit cards are currently accepted, but this policy may change in the future.

Milfred

Tucked away in New England's hills and along its stern and rocky shores are a myriad of quaint, picturesque small towns. One of the region's most typical hamlets is Milfred—a tiny community with a village green encircled by gracious old white houses and a prim needle-spired church, a general store and a modest scattering of shops. It even has a chuckling brook that tumbles helter-skelter over silvery stones; tall, graceful elms shade the town's streets, and beyond the village the countryside stretches for miles marked by stone walls, cool forests of spruce and balsam, and snug New England farms where cattle graze tranquilly upon clover and sweet grass.

Milfred is historic, too. Like many New England towns, it was founded by immigrants from the Old World, back in the late 1600s. Unlike most, however, Milfred was established—not by English or Scottish settlers—but by a small band of Serbian gypsies. It's an unusual tale. The gypsies, as did several other groups of early voyagers, made a slight miscalculation in their travel plans. They had hoped to end up in the Midwest, in Chicago, to be exact. In those days, of course, Chicago was merely a swampy outpost inhabited by Indians and French fur traders. The gypsies hoped to amass great wealth by practicing their traditional skills of sharpening scissors and knives, raising (and occasionally stealing) horses, and telling fortunes.

Unfortunately for their ambitions, the tiny shipload of wanderers misread the charts and traveled too far north. Somewhere at sea they sailed into the path of a violent storm and were wrecked upon the cruel granite coast of Maine. Wet and bedraggled, the brave band struggled ashore. Cursing the evil fate that had not allowed them to make port in Boston or New York (from whence they might wend their way westward) the gypsies decided to make the best of things. Instead of trekking halfway across the continent to another wilderness, they settled for the wilderness they had.

Happily, the newcomers not only managed to survive the inhospitable Maine climate, the savage Indians and a plethora of wolves and mosquitoes, but they actually thrived. The younger ones, at least, abandoned most of their old nomadic gypsy ways and turned to new means of earning a livelihood. They chopped down mighty forests in order to clear farmland; they fished the streams and trapped the beaver; they befriended the local Indians and, in return, the Indians introduced them to New World delicacies such as cranberries, succotash and stewed moose.

But the gypsies never forgot their roots. From the start, the old ones maintained their expertise in fortune-telling, practicing on the Indians at first and later on any stranger who chanced to come their way. And even today the residents of the little town of Milfred still celebrate all festive occasions by dancing 'round a bonfire, the wild and joyous music of fiddle and tambourines still rising through the clear, unpolluted air to astonish the moon riding high above in the midnight-blue sky.

The gypsy citizens of Milfred have also, over the years, become imbued with the traditional values of other New Englanders; in particular, they have learned to fully appreciate the merits of tourism. The one and only hostelry (a rather tacky motel at the edge of town, we're sorry to say) not only was designed to resemble a large tinker's wagon, but has a commodious function room (suitable for conventions) decorated in vivid gypsy colors. Walking tours of the town are offered including one through the historic old houses on the green, and another of the attractive garden district where all the dwellings are mobile homes. An oft-heard Milfred saying is that visitors can easily tell one section of the village from another; the elegant part is where the houses *aren't* on wheels.

The town's shops, though few, are unique. Located in unpretentious storefront quarters along the main street, they all offer spiced tea and in-depth character readings. Locally made crafts are casually displayed, too, including a variety of charms and gaily colored sachets containing oddly scented herbs. For accommodations, there is the motel previously mentioned, or visitors may wish to camp out in the fields beyond the town.

Most Milfred residents speak English nowadays, but not all. As an aid to travelers we are including a few helpful phrases in the native tongue. Two basic sentences will be of great use, we feel: "Govorite li engleski" means "Do you speak English?" and "Ne rasumen" is "I don't understand." Also good to know is "Koliko kosta ovo?" or "How much is this?"; "To je suvise skupo" means "That's too expensive." "Ostacemo samo jednu noc" is "We'll be staying overnight only," and "Moram da idem odmah" means "I've got to leave at once."

Restaurants are somewhat scarce in the Milfred area. We do, however, recommend one in particular, called **Miomir's Serbian Club.** Miomir's menu is authentically ethnic offering such intriguing appetizers as *kajmak*, a fermented milk bread spread originating in the Caucasus, and *ajvar*, a mixture of grilled eggplant, sweet green pepper and celery in olive oil—said to aid long life. Entrees include *lovacka snicla*, (beef in wine sauce), and a number of grilled dishes such as *cevapcici, pleskavica* and *muckalicka. Palacinke*, Serbian crepes, are among the delectable desserts, and for an after-dinner drink we suggest *slivovick*, a lively plum brandy that is served hot and flaming.

Miomir's also provides entertainment, a rousing program of exuberant singing, dancing and music, introduced by the suave and handsome host, Miomir himself. The gypsy patrons, a charmingly friendly lot, will most likely inveigle you onto the dance floor for an energetic round of stomping and twirling. There will also be, on most nights, an old gypsy woman who will read your palm and foretell your future.

Miomir's Serbian Club is, we feel obliged to tell you, a healthy drive from downtown Milfred. It is located at 2255 West Lawrence Avenue, Chicago, Illinois, (312)784-2111, about 900 miles west of Maine. Connecting interstate highways will get you there in about two or three days, or you may choose a more leisurely, roundabout route and follow the old roads. Miomir's hours are from 5 p.m. to around midnight, on Saturdays to 3 a.m.; closed on Monday and Tuesday. Prices are moderate; MasterCard and Visa are accepted.

By now you are undoubtedly wondering exactly where Milfred is, and how you may reach it. To begin with, the town is well off the beaten path—so far off that there are no roads leading in or out, even in summer. In fact, Milfred does

not appear on any map of Maine at all. The only way to find
it is by perseverance, a great deal of serendipity, and sheer
luck. In addition, Milfred suffers from a strange and eery
fate: like Brigadoon, the town appears to outsiders only once
in a very long while—every 33 years, to be precise. This enchantment befell the town long ago when an aged gypsy
crone, irked by an itinerant shoestring salesman who refused
to pay for her predictions, turned the miscreant into a
werewolf and screeched that nevermore (except at designated intervals) would strangers be able to find their way to
Milfred.

We, fortunate travelers that we are, discovered Milfred ac-
cidentally many years ago by our usual method of following
unmarked back-country roads in quest of the odd and
unusual . . . and chancing upon it just at the right time. But
the town's next appearance should be coming up again soon,
so we wish you good fortune and godspeed in your search. If
you do manage to track it down, we're certain that Milfred
will delight you.

Index

Off The Beaten Path in . . .

Off The Beaten Path in . . .

Index

About the Authors

Corinne Madden Ross, the author of *New England: Off The Beaten Path,* is a native New Englander whose appreciation of her home and the pleasures of travel is reflected in her many books, including *The New England Guest House Book* (East Woods Press 1979), *To Market, To Market: Six Walking Tours of the Old and the New Boston* (Charles River Press 1980) and *The Southern Guest House Book* (East Woods Press 1981).

Her collaborator, Ralph Woodward, is a book publishers' representative for the New England states. His broad experience of food and out-of-the-way places in his territory to eat, drink and be merry has added weight to the recommendations (and to the authors) of *New England: Off The Beaten Path.*

East Woods Press Books

Backcountry Cooking by J. Wayne Fears
The Complete Guide to Backpacking in Canada by Elliott Katz
Florida By Paddle and Pack by Mike Toner and Pat Toner
The Fructose Cookbook by Minuha Cannon
The Grand Strand by Nancy Rhyne
The Healthy Trail Food Book by Dorcas S. Miller
Honky Tonkin' by Richard Wootton
Hosteling USA by Michael Frome
Inside Outward Bound by Renate Wilson
Just Folks by Jerry Bledsoe
Kays Gary, Columnist edited by C.A. McKnight
The Living Land by Marguerite Schumann
The Maine Coast by Dorcas S. Miller
The New England Guest House Book by Corinne Madden Ross
New England: Off the Beaten Path
    by Corinne Madden Ross and Ralph Woodward
Parent Power! by John K. Rosemond
Roxy's Ski Guide to New England by Roxy Rothafel
Sea Islands of the South by Diana and Bill Gleasner
The Southern Guest House Book by Corinne Madden Ross
Steppin' Out by Susanne Weil and Barry Singer
Sweets Without Guilt by Minuha Cannon
Train Trips by William G. Scheller
Trout Fishing the Southern Appalachians by J. Wayne Fears
Vacationer's Guide to Orlando and Central Florida
    by Judi Foster Grove
Walks With Nature in Rocky Mountain National Park
    by Kent and Donna Dannen
Wild Places of the South by Steve Price
You Can't Live On Radishes by Jerry Bledsoe

PT261   655

LIBRARY OF DAVIDSON COLLEGE

Books on regular loan may be checked out for **two weeks**. Books must be presented at the Circulation Desk in order to be renewed.

A fine is charged after date due.

Special books are subject to special regulations at the discretion of the library staff.

JUL 16 1986